ALEXANDER HAMILTON

TIME

Published by Liberty Street,
a division of Meredith Corporation
225 Liberty Street
New York, NY 10281

ISBN: 978-1-68330-075-5
Library of Congress Control Number: 2018931948

First edition, 2018
1 QGV 18
10 9 8 7 6 5 4 3 2 1

We welcome your comments and suggestions about Time Inc. Books.
Please write to us at:

Time Inc. Books
Attention: Book Editors
P.O. Box 62310
Tampa, FL 33662-2310
(800) 765-6400

timeincbooks.com

Time Inc. Books products may be purchased for business or promotional
use. For information on bulk purchases, please contact Christi Crowley in
the Special Sales Department at (845) 895-9858.

HEROES OF HISTORY

ALEXANDER HAMILTON

Contents

In which we meet our hero—at the very end of his journey.

The sun hadn't yet risen on the morning of July 11, 1804, when two rowboats set out from the island of Manhattan. It began to peek above the horizon as the boats made their way through the early morning mist toward the New Jersey shore. One boat carried a doctor, a man named Nathaniel Pendleton, and a former secretary of the treasury. In the other rode a lawyer named William P. Van Ness and the vice president of the United States. All were bound for a bluff in Weehawken, New Jersey.

Vice President Aaron Burr got there first. Former secretary Alexander Hamilton—revolutionary, framer of the Constitution, and architect of the American economy—arrived soon after.

THE FATAL DUEL, SHOWN HERE IN AN ETCHING FROM 1905, WOULD CAPTURE AMERICANS' IMAGINATIONS FOR CENTURIES TO COME.

Their seconds, the men they had chosen to support them in the duel, cleared the area of brush and paced out a field. The two duelers each took a weapon—a heavy wooden flintlock pistol—and faced off across the clearing. In minutes, it was over. Aaron Burr escaped unscathed. Alexander Hamilton lay mortally wounded.

Their duel would become the most famous in American history. Even before Hamilton had died of his wounds, the city of New York was buzzing with the news. It brought the vice president's

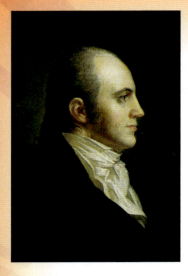

political career to a screeching halt and sent him into hiding. It would become a part of American culture, inspiring books, a musical, and even television commercials centuries later.

It was the last chapter in the story of Alexander Hamilton's life, but it was hardly the first time he had caused a stir. Hamilton was a man of extremes. Always sure that he was right, he charged headfirst into battles without looking back, sometimes with disastrous results. Desperate to make a name for himself, and to protect that name, he entangled himself in countless disputes. His duel with Aaron Burr had been not his first duel but his eleventh. Powerhouse that he was, Hamilton was often his own worst enemy.

Yet he had an enormous influence on the young United States. A fervent nationalist and the country's first secretary of the treasury, he brought order to

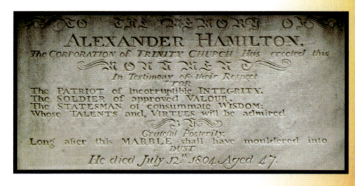

HAMILTON'S GRAVESTONE AT TRINITY CHURCH, NEW YORK, PAYS TRIBUTE TO HIM AS A PATRIOT, SOLDIER, AND STATESMAN.

the new republic's finances, earned it credit at home and abroad, and strengthened the national government, setting constitutional precedents that persist today.

A skilled wordsmith, Hamilton poured himself into his writings. He defended the Constitution, the national government, and his own reputation with fervor. In moments of crisis, though, Hamilton could push too hard, say too much, and compromise too little. He was intolerant of opposition. More than once, he favored military solutions to domestic crises in the hopes of quashing resistance to government authority.

In the confusion of the republic's founding, with no precise model to follow, Hamilton declared himself the man with the answers. As polarizing as his politics were—and indeed, they divided the country—they triggered an important conversation about the nation's destiny. In the push and pull of devising a new government, someone had to start things off and stake a claim. Hamilton was that man.

AN OUTPOURING OF GRIEF FOLLOWED HAMILTON'S DEATH. THIS ARTICLE, DESCRIBING HIS FUNERAL, APPEARED IN THE NEW-YORK EVENING POST ON JULY 17, 1804.

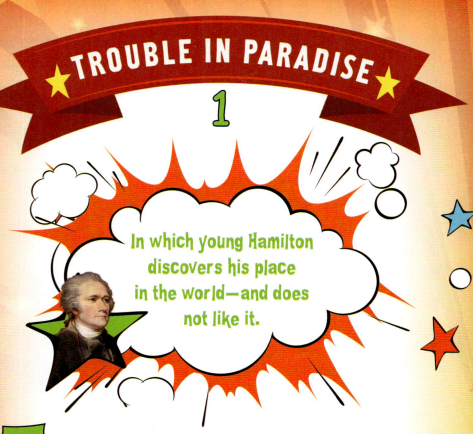

★ TROUBLE IN PARADISE ★

1

In which young Hamilton discovers his place in the world—and does not like it.

The Caribbean island of Nevis isn't the first place you'd think to look for one of America's Founding Fathers. An oval speck with a volcanic peak at its center, it is one of the Leeward Islands, a series of islands that rings the eastern edge of the Caribbean Sea. Nevis is a tropical paradise, with towering waterfalls, lush gorges, and hot sulfur springs. Its dense rain forests swarm with Antillean crested hummingbirds and Pallas's mastiff bats—not to mention the descendants of the African vervet monkeys

1755
BORN ON THE ISLAND OF NEVIS

1765
MOVED TO ST. CROIX

PINNEY'S BEACH, NEVIS, TODAY WITH ST. KITTS IN THE DISTANCE.

1768
RACHEL
FAUCETTE LAVIEN
DIED

1772
SENT
TO AMERICA

11

that were brought ashore by French settlers in the 17th century. The turquoise waters that lap against the island's sandy beaches are home to spiny lobsters, green turtles, and spinner dolphins.

Yet it was on Nevis, in the harbor town of Charlestown, that Alexander Hamilton was born. And it was on Nevis and the neighboring island of St. Croix that he endured the harsh childhood that steeled him for the high-stakes battles that awaited him as an adult.

Alexander Hamilton's mother, Rachel Faucette, was born on Nevis around 1729. Her parents, John and Mary, owned a plantation on which they grew sugar, the "white gold" that made that part of the world so prosperous. By the 18th century, the island was a melting pot of treasure seekers. John was French Huguenot and Mary was British, but Nevis also welcomed an assortment of Irish, Jewish, and Spanish residents. All of them were wealthy planters and merchants. But the sugar colonies were also a human dumping ground for the British, a place to exile criminals such as thieves.

A PHOTO TAKEN IN THE LATE 1800S SHOWS A TYPICAL SUGAR ESTATE ON NEVIS.

Like other Caribbean islands that thrived on the sugar crop—and many areas in North America at the time—the island of Nevis relied on slave labor to keep its plantations running. Ships packed with shackled Africans arrived regularly in Charlestown's harbor. Before long, the island's 1,000 white citizens were outnumbered four to one, then eight to one, by its enslaved people.

Diseases such as yellow fever, malaria, and dysentery periodically ravaged the community, and five of Rachel's six siblings died young. So after her father breathed his last in 1745, she inherited what her famous son would one day call "a *snug* fortune." After burying her father, she took her inheritance and her mother 140 miles west to Christiansted, on the island of St. Croix.

Wherever she landed, the smart and pretty 16-year-old was going to be a valuable catch. Unfortunately, the eye she caught belonged to Johann Michael Lavien, a ne'er-do-well 30-year-old Dane, who saw a wife with an inheritance as a shortcut to his dream of becoming a successful planter. The couple settled on Lavien's plantation—Contentment—but despite the name, the union did not work out. They had a child, Peter, but Lavien was an inept businessman and squandered his wife's money. It was, as Alexander Hamilton later described it, "a hated marriage."

Around 1750, Rachel left the marriage. Enraged by the affront, Lavien set off a chain of events that would forever taint Rachel and her future children. Danish law at the time gave a husband the right to imprison an adulterous, deserting wife. On false accusations, Rachel was imprisoned in the town fort. She spent months in a small cell, surviving on salted herring, cornmeal mush, and cod. In the end, however, the experience didn't break her. When she was released, Rachel sailed with her mother to the island of St. Kitts.

She hadn't been there long before she met James Hamilton. On first impression, he seemed to be the exact opposite of Johann Lavien. James was well born. His father, Alexander, was the laird of Grange in the county of Ayrshire, in southwestern Scotland. James had left the family castle in 1741 to seek his fortune across the ocean. Lacking both business sense and industriousness, though, he was struggling by the time he met Rachel on St. Kitts. Divorce from her previous husband was not an option, so Rachel and James entered into a common-law marriage, addressed as Mr.

and Mrs. James Hamilton even though it was well known that Rachel was another man's wife. James, Jr., arrived in 1753. By the time Alexander was born, on January 11, 1755, the family had relocated to Nevis.

The wooden buildings and narrow streets of Charlestown bustled with merchants and traders, pirates and old salts. From his home, the young Alexander—remembered by a mentor as "rather delicate & frail"—could hear the buzz of

HAMILTON'S BIRTHPLACE TODAY.

15

FORT CHRISTIANSVÆRN DOMINATED THE COASTLINE OF CHRISTIANSTED, ON THE ISLAND OF ST. CROIX.

the docks as cargo was unloaded and deals were struck. But he did not feel welcome there. His parents' unofficial marriage meant that the handsome boy with the red hair and the piercing violet eyes was viewed as a bastard child. His illegitimacy racked him throughout his life. "My birth is the subject of the most humiliating criticism," he reluctantly admitted in later years. The stigma permeated his life. Alexander was taught by a tutor at home—likely because he wasn't allowed to attend an Anglican school.

In 1759, when Alexander was 4, Rachel's marriage to Lavien

finally came to an official end. Looking to remarry, Lavien began divorce proceedings. He accused Rachel of having "completely forgotten her duty" by abandoning her one legitimate child. Lavien got his divorce, and in the process, the court also denied Rachel the right to remarry.

A few years later, James landed a job as head clerk for a tobacco merchant on St. Croix, and he moved the family to Christiansted. Soon after, though, he abandoned his wife and sons. Alexander never saw his father again, and he received no response after inviting the man to his wedding in 1780.

Rachel was left to raise her boys alone in a community well aware of her reputation, however unfairly it was gained. Christiansted was not a large city; one's social station was plainly evident for others to see.

Rachel did her best, but, abandoned and scorned, she inevitably found herself in need of some help. She received it from her sister's husband, James Lytton, who paid the rent on their two-story house. Rachel and the boys lived on the second floor. They kept a goat in the yard, and Alexander, an avid reader, shelved his books in their rooms. Rachel ran a general store out of the first floor, where she sold beef, salted fish, flour, rice, and other supplies that she bought from her landlord and from two New York merchants, David Beekman and Nicholas Cruger, who ran a trading firm on the island. Rachel owned five female slaves and their children, and she rented them out when she was short of money. The Hamiltons weren't exactly the privileged class, but they were making their way.

Then, in early 1768, both Alexander and Rachel came down with a fever. They shared a sickbed. Doctors came to visit, but medicine of the time often did more harm than good. One doctor bled Alexander, slicing open veins with a blade to rebalance his body's "humors." Rachel was prescribed medicine to make her vomit and an herbal remedy with laxative properties. Mother and son, withering from these useless and energy-draining treatments, lay side by side. Alexander recovered. Rachel did not. She died on February 19.

Because she was a divorced woman, the church likely denied Rachel a proper funeral, which might be why she was laid to rest on her sister and brother-in-law's estate. Making matters worse for her essentially orphaned children, Lavien reappeared, insisting that Peter, the son he had with Rachel, was her sole heir. Rachel didn't have much, but what she did own, Lavien argued successfully, was now Peter's. James and Alexander were disinherited. The impoverished Hamilton boys were taken in by their cousin, Peter Lytton, James Lytton's son—but in quick succession, both Lyttons died, too.

Fortunately for Alexander, he was taken in by another local merchant, Thomas Stevens, and his wife. One of the couple's five children, Edward, became Alexander's closest friend. In fact, the two shared an uncanny resemblance that led many to believe that the elder Stevens was Alexander's actual father—a fact that, if true, would explain why he had so readily welcomed the young teen into his home.

Though the vengeful Lavien had snatched away Rachel's few material possessions, Hamilton definitely came away with her smarts. And,

THOUGH LAVIEN HAD SNATCHED AWAY RACHEL'S FEW POSSESSIONS, HAMILTON CAME AWAY WITH HER SMARTS.

at last secure, ensconced in a proper new home and a challenging new job, the 14-year-old began to blossom. As Stevens's apprentice, Hamilton dove headfirst into a world of multinational commerce. In the 18th century, the islands of the Caribbean were the crossroads of empires, where European powers competed with one another to enrich themselves through the trade of commodities and enslaved people. They were also a place where a boy of Hamilton's social standing was able to see firsthand the grinding poverty that an agricultural economy forced on people. The vast slave class, without which extracting sugar and other resources from the land would not have been profitable, suffered the most.

Hamilton was transformed. He learned to write clearly and balance books. He polished his French (which his mother had taught him) and handled foreign currencies: British pounds, Dutch stivers, Spanish pieces of eight, and Danish ducats. He sorted through inventories, negotiated with crusty ship captains, and cracked the secrets of traders and smugglers alike. Later, Hamilton would refer to his time at the merchants' house as "the most useful" of his education.

Beekman and Cruger owned a shop and a warehouse in town as well as a dock and a ship. Their firm supplied local planters with the products they needed: flour, rice, timber, beer, beef, cider,

HAMILTON'S JOURNEY NORTH WAS UNDERWRITTEN BY LOCAL MERCHANTS INCLUDING NICHOLAS CRUGER.

mules, and cattle. It also dealt in slaves, transporting hundreds of enslaved people to the islands. Hamilton had to appraise the new arrivals. This was one part of the job he did not enjoy. He saw the injustice of the slave trade up close, and he would become an early abolitionist.

As he became acquainted with the world beyond the Leeward Islands, Hamilton began to imagine greater adventures and glory for himself.

In November 1769, he wrote to his friend Edward, who had headed off to King's College in New York City, of his frustrations: "Ned, my Ambition is [so] prevalent that I contemn the grov'ling and condition of a Clerk or the like, to which my Fortune &c. condemns me and would willingly risk my life tho' not my Character to exalt my Station." The young Hamilton knew that one sure way for a man like himself to improve his social standing was to serve with distinction in the military. He finished his letter, "I shall Conclude [by] saying I wish there was a War."

Hamilton, an unfulfilled romantic, began writing poetry as an outlet for his longing. The island's *Royal Danish American Gazette* published Hamilton's precocious verse about love and religion. He also fell under the tutelage of the Reverend Hugh Knox, the minister of the local Scotch Presbyterian church and a part-time editor at the *Gazette*. Knox guided the bookish young man's education, offering him access to his library and influencing him with his liberal views, including an opposition to slavery. The 17-year-old might not have been satisfied by the life he had carved out for himself, but from the outside, he looked very much like what he was: one of the town's up-and-coming merchant clerks.

On August 31, 1772, a devastating storm tore through the Caribbean. What the *Gazette* called "the most dreadful Hurricane known in the memory of man" raged unabated over St. Croix for six hours, destroying homes and refineries, ripping up trees, flattening cane fields, and sweeping away boats. A massive storm

Alexander Hamilton and Slavery

Growing up among sugar plantations, Hamilton saw firsthand the injustice and brutality of slavery. In 1785, he, New York governor George Clinton, future Supreme Court chief justice John Jay, and others founded what they called the "New-York Society for Promoting the Manumission of Slaves, and Protecting Such of Them as Have Been, or May Be Liberated." The men hoped to "excite the indignation of every friend to humanity" and sought to ban slavery. Somewhat awkwardly, many of the society's members themselves owned slaves; Hamilton proposed a bold plan outlining a specific schedule of manumission, or emancipation, for members' slaves, but this was voted down as too extreme. Still, the group advocated for those with no rights. The members published essays attacking the slave trade, and opened the African Free School, which offered an education to black children. The society was among the antislavery organizations that petitioned Congress in 1791 to limit the trade in enslaved people, and though the effort failed, it paved the way for a 1799 law that was the first step toward the later law that freed all of New York's enslaved people by 1827.

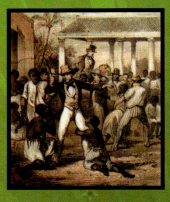

AN ENGRAVING FROM 1858 DEPICTS ONE OF THE MANY TRAGEDIES OF SLAVERY: A MAN BEING SEPARATED FROM HIS SON AND DAUGHTER.

THIS SET OF ANKLE SHACKLES FROM THE 19TH CENTURY ARE SIMILAR TO THOSE WORN BY MANY ENSLAVED PEOPLE.

surge pummeled the island. Once the sky cleared, Hamilton wrote a letter to his father describing what had happened. Before sending it, he showed it to Knox, who encouraged him to have it published.

Hamilton's recounting of the hurricane appeared in the *Gazette* on October 3. It read, in part: "The roaring of the sea and wind, fiery meteors flying about it in the air, the prodigious glare of almost perpetual lightning, the crash of the falling houses, and the ear-piercing shrieks of the distressed, were sufficient to strike astonishment into Angels. A great part of the buildings throughout the Island are levelled to the ground, almost all the rest very much shattered; several persons killed and numbers utterly ruined; whole families running about the streets, unknowing where to find a place of shelter; the sick exposed to the keeness of water and air without a bed to lie upon, or a dry covering to their bodies; and our harbours entirely bare. In a word, misery, in all its most hideous shapes, spread over the whole face of the country." The published letter immediately revealed the scholarship and ability of this uncanny youth to all on the island, from the governor on down. A collection was taken up to help send Hamilton to America, where he could get a proper education. Within months, he was boarding a boat and bidding goodbye to the only world he knew.

"The changes in the human conditions are uncertain and frequent," he would note 16 years later, during a debate over the adoption of the U.S. Constitution. "Many, on whom fortune has bestowed her favours, may trace their family to a more unprosperous

THIS EARLY PORTRAIT OF HAMILTON WAS CREATED AROUND THE TIME HE ARRIVED IN AMERICA.

station; and many who are now in obscurity, may look back upon the affluence and exalted rank of their ancestors." But when he set sail that day, he could have no idea of what awaited him in the British colonies of North America. He knew only that he had been given a chance to challenge the presumed fate of a child born to a woman wrongly judged.

Fortunately, as his ship slipped from the harbor of St. Croix, he carried with him more than his few earthly belongings. He also carried the gifts left to him by his mother: an extraordinary drive and a Herculean will, both of which he would have to call upon again and again as he joined the fight to mold a new nation.

Lighting the Way for Sailors

As his storm-tossed brig passed North Carolina's Cape Hatteras on the way to New York in the early 1770s, a fearful Hamilton vowed to someday build a way-finding lighthouse there. In 1789, Congress passed "An Act for the establishment and support of Lighthouses, Beacons, Buoys, and Public Piers," and the job of maintaining those structures was given to the Department of the Treasury. Thus Hamilton found himself the "superintendent" of lighthouses. His first commission, which rose near the entrance to the Chesapeake Bay, was designed by John McComb, Jr., who would one day build the Grange, Hamilton's New York home. And in 1803 a promise was kept, as "Mr. Hamilton's Light" opened on Cape Hatteras.

HAMILTON'S LIGHTHOUSE AT CAPE HATTERAS WAS REBUILT AFTER THE ORIGINAL SUCCUMBED TO EROSION.

The West Indies During the Revolutionary War

IN ADDITION TO THE 13 COLONIES IN NORTH AMERICA, BRITAIN HAD 13 OTHER COLONIES IN THE NEW WORLD. THE BRITISH WEST INDIES INCLUDED BELIZE (IN CENTRAL AMERICA), THE BAHAMAS, BARBADOS, AND BERMUDA, AS WELL AS THE SMALLER ISLANDS OF THE WINDWARD AND LEEWARD ISLAND CHAINS.

NEVIS

NEVIS WAS PART OF THE LEEWARD ISLANDS, AND LIKE THE REST OF THE BRITISH COLONIES IN THE CARIBBEAN, IT REMAINED LOYAL TO BRITAIN WHEN AMERICA DECLARED ITS INDEPENDENCE. LIKE THE 13 AMERICAN COLONIES, THE CARIBBEAN ISLANDS WERE TAXED SEVERELY. TARIFFS UNDER THE STAMP ACT OF 1765 WERE HIGHER FOR COLONIES IN THE WEST INDIES THAN THEY WERE FOR THOSE IN AMERICA.

THE STAMP ACT WAS UNPOPULAR THROUGHOUT THE COLONIES. ABOVE A PROTEST STAMP.

BRITISH COLONIAL FEARS OF A SLAVE REVOLT WERE REALIZED IN 1831 IN JAMAICA. AS MANY AS 60,000 ENSLAVED PEOPLE FOUGHT BACK IN THE CHRISTMAS REBELLION (ALSO KNOWN AS THE BAPTIST WAR).

BUT THE WEST INDIES RELIED ON BRITAIN IN A WAY THAT THE AMERICAN COLONIES DID NOT. THE SUGAR CROP THAT DROVE THE ISLANDS RELIED HEAVILY ON SLAVE LABOR. AS MANY AS 90% OF THE RESIDENTS OF THE ISLANDS WERE ENSLAVED AFRICANS, AND WHITE PLANTATION OWNERS LIVED IN FEAR OF REBELLION. THEY WELCOMED THE PRESENCE OF THE BRITISH ARMY—EACH ISLAND HAD A FORT AND BARRACKS FOR SOLDIERS. THE ISLANDS ALSO RELIED ON THE BRITISH MARKET, THE LARGEST IN THE WORLD FOR SUGAR, TO TRADE THEIR PRIMARY CROP.

AS THE REVOLUTIONARY WAR HEATED UP, THE CARIBBEAN BECAME AN IMPORTANT FRONT. WHEN FRANCE SENT SHIPS TO SUPPORT THE CONTINENTAL ARMY IN 1778, THE FLEET, UNDER THE COMMAND OF CHARLES—HECTOR, COUNT D'ESTAING, SOON LEFT AMERICA TO DEFEND THE FRENCH CARIBBEAN ISLANDS. LORD CORNWALLIS HAD HOPED FOR BRITISH SUPPORT FROM THE SEA DURING THE BATTLE OF YORKTOWN, BUT THE SHIPS, BUSY DEFENDING THE COLONIES IN THE WEST INDIES, DID NOT ARRIVE.

FRANÇOIS—JOSEPH—PAUL, COUNT DE GRASSE, WHO LED THE FRENCH FLEET TO VICTORY AT THE BATTLE OF THE CHESAPEAKE DURING THE REVOLUTIONARY WAR, WAS DEFEATED IN THE CARIBBEAN BY BRITISH ADMIRAL GEORGE RODNEY IN THE BATTLE OF THE SAINTES LESS THAN A YEAR LATER.

THE CARIBBEAN COLONIES, DOWN TO STARVATION RATIONS AS THEY STRUGGLED TO SUPPLY BRITISH TROOPS IN THE WAR, WERE FLOODED WITH LOYALISTS FLEEING THE CONFLICT IN AMERICA. THE WEST INDIES WOULD REMAIN FAITHFUL TO BRITAIN FOR CENTURIES TO COME.

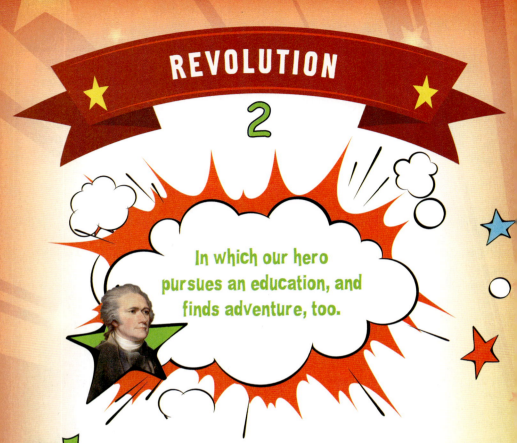

In which our hero pursues an education, and finds adventure, too.

Hamilton's journey north to his new life was by no means smooth sailing: his ship caught fire at sea, and it took a day to douse the flames. After three hard weeks, the damaged brig finally arrived at Boston Harbor, Massachusetts. Hamilton immediately headed south to see about entering the College of New Jersey (later called Princeton University). His previous education being haphazard at best, he knew he needed to prepare for the entrance exam, so he enrolled at the Elizabethtown Academy

1773
ENROLLED AT KING'S COLLEGE

1773
BOSTON TEA PARTY

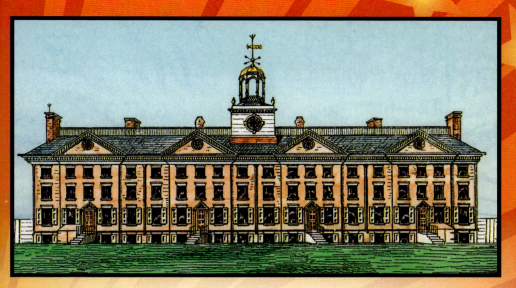

in Elizabethtown, New Jersey, to bone up on Latin and Greek. The extra work did the trick: he aced the test.

But according to a friend, Hercules Mulligan, the college was not in favor of Hamilton's intention to finish "with as much rapidity as his exertions would enable him to do." At the time, the colonies were home to just eight other colleges. But Hamilton didn't have to look far for a second choice. Back across the Hudson River stood King's College.

In the early 1770s, some 25,000 people lived on Manhattan Island, most on its developed southern end. The multilingual city on the harbor boasted a growing merchant class, a volatile political

1775
BATTLES OF
LEXINGTON AND
CONCORD

1776
ENLISTED
AS AN ARTILLERY
COMPANY CAPTAIN

29

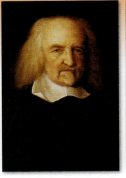

AS A STUDENT, HAMILTON STUDIED THE WORKS OF GREAT POLITICAL PHILOSOPHERS. FROM LEFT TO RIGHT: JOHN LOCKE, THOMAS HOBBES, DAVID HUME, AND MONTESQUIEU.

climate, and combative newspapers. It was a place where Hamilton would not only fit in but also blossom.

He entered King's College in late 1773 or early 1774. The school, which after the revolution would be renamed Columbia College, occupied a single building in a meadow overlooking the river. Along with 16 other students, Hamilton wore a cap and gown and studied the classics, geography, philosophy, math, science, and rhetoric. He dove into the political philosophies of John Locke, Thomas Hobbes, David Hume, Montesquieu, and others. But even as he crammed to make up for lost classroom time, he also took part in extracurricular literary societies and helped found a club in which students discussed politics and honed their writing and public speaking skills. In that club, according to his friend Robert Troup, Hamilton "made extraordinary displays of richness of genius and energy of mind."

King's College was run by Loyalists, people who supported British rule in the colonies. It was a conservative institution with an Anglican minister, Myles Cooper, in charge. That, too, suited

Hamilton—as a child of the Caribbean, he had already sworn allegiance to the monarchy, so the school felt like home. But the fence that surrounded it was not nearly tall enough to keep out the intruder that was closing in. Down the road, on the grassy field that was known as the Commons, a pole supported a gilded weather vane. At the top was the word **LIBERTY**.

Even before Hamilton arrived on the mainland, the colonists had been agitating. Much of the strain grew out of Britain's decision to tax the colonies to help resolve its financial problems. The costly French and Indian War, which had ended in 1763, had helped push Britain's national debt so high that half the government's annual budget was devoted to interest payments. Reasoning that the American colonists had benefited from the war, Parliament turned to them to help cover its costs.

First came the Stamp Act of 1765, which imposed a tax on legal documents, newspapers, and even playing cards. To many Americans, this was a plain violation of the long tradition that only their own legislatures could impose taxes on them. The Stamp Act set off a storm of protest, and Parliament repealed it just one year later, only to revive the controversy a year after that with the passage of the Townshend Acts. These placed heavy duties on a range of British imports,

UNDER THE STAMP ACT, NEWSPAPERS AND DOCUMENTS HAD TO BE PRINTED ON STAMPED PAPER BOUGHT FROM BRITAIN.

including paint, paper, glass, and tea. Colonists resented the restrictions on self-rule—not to mention the unfair taxes—imposed by the Stamp Act and the Townshend Acts. In January 1770, members of the colonial underground, known as the Sons of Liberty, scuffled with British troops in the Battle of Golden Hill, resulting in a number of injuries. Two months later, on March 5, a bloodier confrontation broke out. Protesting the Townshend Acts and urging a boycott, five colonists were killed in what would become known as the Boston Massacre.

Then, on December 16, 1773, Boston patriots dressed as Mohawk Indians dumped £9,659 (equivalent to about $1.7 million

A 19TH-CENTURY ENGRAVING SHOWS PATRIOTS DRESSED AS AMERICAN INDIANS BREAKING INTO CRATES HOLDING TEA DURING THE BOSTON TEA PARTY.

today) of tea in their harbor to protest a tax on the kitchen staple. Intrigued by the unrest, Hamilton took a trip to Boston, and upon his return he wrote a piece for the *New-York Journal*, "Defence and Destruction of the Tea." Meanwhile, in retaliation for the turmoil, Parliament imposed the Coercive Acts, which shuttered Boston's port and enforced military rule, among other penalties. The colonists referred to these as the Intolerable Acts. Far from cowing the colonists, the new laws spurred a total embargo of British goods.

It was all an exciting distraction for a political-minded student. Throughout New York, patriots posted broadsides and handbills, circulated petitions, and staged rallies. The Sons of Liberty held one such event on the Commons on July 6, 1774. Hamilton, whose views on British rule were rapidly changing, stepped up to voice support for the Boston Tea Party and the boycott, predicting that they would "prove the salvation of North America and her liberties." His speech drew enthusiastic applause.

Not everyone, however, embraced the defiance. At King's College, President Cooper smeared the Sons of Liberty as "sons of licentiousness." And a Loyalist reverend, Samuel Seabury, branded the members of that fall's First Continental Congress "a venomous brood of scorpions." Hamilton could not let Seabury's slanderous writing pass. He wrote a 35-page rebuttal,

REVEREND SAMUEL SEABURY

A PAINTING FROM THE MID—1800S DEPICTS THE MOMENT WAR BROKE OUT ON LEXINGTON GREEN, APRIL 19, 1775.

A Full Vindication of the Measures of the Congress, that revealed its 19-year-old author to have an uncanny knowledge of politics, British law, history, and philosophy. When Seabury responded, Hamilton penned the even longer *The Farmer Refuted*. It was written with what would become his trademark one-two punch: slashing accusation and glib articulation of issues. Hamilton called the minister's charges "puerile and fallacious" and argued that the colonists had the power "to harass and exhaust the soldiery" until there was a peace.

Soon after, war broke out. On April 19, 1775, British redcoats, on their way to seize the colonists' military stores in Concord, Massachusetts, passed through the nearby town of Lexington. There, they were met by 77 colonial militiamen—called minutemen—and other volunteers on the local green. Shots were exchanged, and the colonists retreated. Later, "the shot heard round the world" was fired at Concord as a few hundred Americans attacked the British.

Once word of the open rebellion trickled south, New Yorkers "paraded the town with drums beating and colours flying," wrote Judge Thomas Jones. The Sons of Liberty seized 1,000 weapons from the city hall's arsenal. Militias sprang up, and Hamilton joined one called the Hearts of Oak (alternatively known as the Corsicans). But even as he brimmed with revolutionary fervor and read up on military tactics, he could not embrace mob rule. On May 10, hundreds of townspeople descended on King's College, intent on tarring and feathering its Loyalist president. According to

Robert Troup, Hamilton "instantly resolved to take his stand on the stairs in front of the Doctor's apartment." He berated the crowd, holding them off long enough for Cooper to climb the school's fence and flee.

That same day, the Second Continental Congress met in the Pennsylvania State House (better known today as Independence Hall) to appoint then-Colonel George Washington commander in chief of the Continental Army.

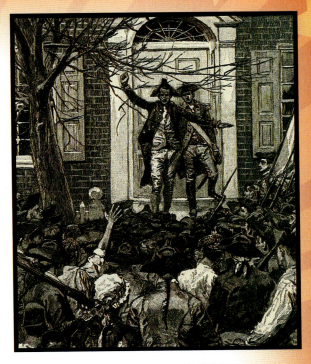

AN ENGRAVING FROM 1884 DEPICTS HAMILTON DELAYING THE MOB ON THE STEPS OF KING'S COLLEGE.

Earlier that month, H.M.S. *Asia*, a British 64-gun man-of-war, had sailed into New York Harbor. And on June 17, 1775, the revolution's first real combat—the Battle of Bunker Hill—took place. By August, King George III was forced to recognize that his colonies had "at length proceeded to open and avowed rebellion."

With the *Asia* anchored offshore, the patriots feared that the British might try to seize the cannons at Fort George, on

LARGE ENOUGH TO CARRY 64 GUNS (CANNONS) BUT SMALL ENOUGH TO BE AGILE, THE *ASIA* WAS A FORMIDABLE SIGHT OFF THE COAST OF THE MASSACHUSETTS SHORE.

Manhattan's southern tip. So Hamilton and 15 of his classmates set out to move the weaponry to safety. "I recollect well that Mr. Hamilton was there," wrote Hercules Mulligan, "for I was engaged in hauling off one of the cannon when Mr. H. came up and gave me his musket to hold and he took hold of the rope." As they carried out the mission, soldiers on a barge launched from the *Asia* shot at them. When Hamilton and the others returned fire, the warship shot off a barrage of cannonballs and grapeshot. The revolutionaries got away, unscathed, with the cannons and dragged them uptown to the Commons.

Between late 1775 and the start of 1776, Hamilton wrote a series of pieces about the growing tensions for the *New-York Journal*. Meanwhile, a little-known immigrant from Thetford, England, Thomas Paine, printed a 50-page pamphlet, *Common Sense*, that mocked monarchy. "One of the strongest *natural* proofs of the folly of hereditary right in kings, is, that nature disapproves it, otherwise she

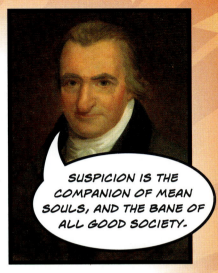

SUSPICION IS THE COMPANION OF MEAN SOULS, AND THE BANE OF ALL GOOD SOCIETY.

THOMAS PAINE

would not so frequently turn it into ridicule by giving mankind an *ass for a lion*," Paine wrote. His appeal for independence quickly sold 500,000 copies and galvanized Americans.

Those Americans continued to terrorize New York's remaining Loyalists. Hamilton, now 21, put the finishing touches on his 14th essay for the *Journal*, then joined the Continental Army. With his transformation to soldier complete, he wanted to make sure that those living in his old homeland understood the depth of his commitment: "I was born to die and my reason and conscience tell me it is impossible to die in a better or more important cause," he wrote in one of his regular reports to the *Royal Danish American Gazette* in St. Croix.

THOMAS PAINE'S PAMPHLET WON MANY TO THE CAUSE OF INDEPENDENCE.

With New York under siege, the rebels closed off streets, threw up defensive batteries, and shut down King's College. In March 1776, Hamilton became a captain in the army, charged with raising an artillery company. Among his duties was overseeing the construction of a fort just northeast of the Commons. In June, Captain Hamilton led 100 men against a British-controlled lighthouse at Sandy Hook, on the coast of New Jersey. Unfortunately, the British were ready for them. Hamilton regretted that his men "could make no impression on the walls."

The shadow of full British might finally darkened the horizon on June 29. As a rifleman named Daniel McCurtin looked out over New York Harbor, he was stunned to see 110 ships, transporting 9,000 troops led by General William Howe and Admiral Richard Howe: "I declare that I thought all London was afloat." With some 20,000 soldiers under his command, General Washington bemoaned his position. Recognizing that they were "extremely deficient in Arms," he had them melt down roof and window lead for bullets. Days later, on July 4, the Continental Congress announced "the unanimous Declaration of the thirteen united States of America"—the Declaration of Independence.

Four years earlier, a hurricane had swept Hamilton off St. Croix. Now another storm was gathering force off the coast of his new home, soon to make landfall. Hamilton had always dreamed of waging war. That dream was about to come true.

HAMILTON HAD ALWAYS DREAMED OF WAGING WAR. THAT DREAM WAS ABOUT TO COME TRUE.

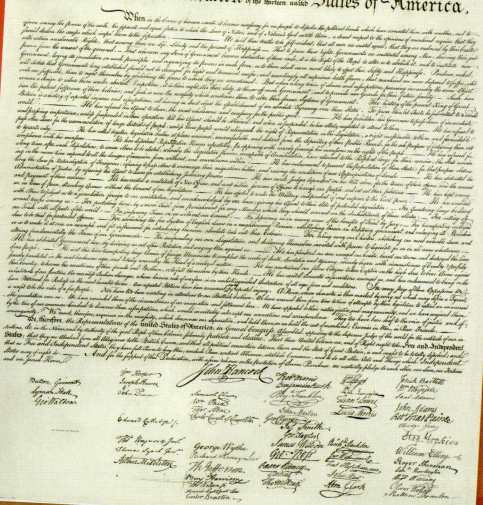

THE DECLARATION OF INDEPENDENCE, HOUSED TODAY AT THE NATIONAL ARCHIVES IN WASHINGTON, D.C., RELAYED A LIST OF REASONS WHY THE AMERICAN COLONIES NEEDED TO BE FREE OF BRITISH RULE.

Two Hundred Years of Heroism

AMERICA'S FOUNDING FATHERS ENJOY A SPECIAL PLACE IN AMERICANS' HEARTS. GEORGE WASHINGTON IS BELOVED FOR HIS MORAL AUTHORITY, AND BENJAMIN FRANKLIN FOR HIS SMARTS. BUT ALEXANDER HAMILTON IS SOMETHING ALTOGETHER DIFFERENT. TODAY IT IS HIS RAKISH ADVENTURING THAT CONTINUES TO DRAW FANS.

LIN-MANUEL MIRANDA (CENTER) WROTE *HAMILTON* WITH THE HELP OF HISTORIAN RON CHERNOW.

IT WAS HAMILTON'S ORIGINS AS A POOR BOY GROWING UP ON A CARIBBEAN ISLAND THAT APPEALED TO THE CREATOR OF THE MUSICAL *HAMILTON*, LIN-MANUEL MIRANDA. WORKING WITH RON CHERNOW, A HISTORIAN WHO WROTE A BESTSELLING BIOGRAPHY OF HAMILTON, MIRANDA WROTE A GROUNDBREAKING MUSICAL THAT BLENDED RAP AND HIP-HOP WITH HISTORY. IT WAS A HIT, WINNING 11 TONYS AND A PULITZER PRIZE FOR DRAMA, AND PLAYING TO SOLD-OUT CROWDS FOR MONTHS.

FROM LEFT TO RIGHT: DAVEED DIGGS, OKIERIETE ONAODOWAN, ANTHONY RAMOS, AND MIRANDA TAKE THE STAGE IN THE ORIGINAL PRODUCTION OF *HAMILTON*.

HAMILTON *SPARKED* A WAVE OF HAMILTONMANIA, BUT THE MAN IT DESCRIBES MAY BE MORE OF A HERO FOR THE 21ST CENTURY THAN AN ACCURATELY PORTRAYED 18TH-CENTURY FIGURE. HISTORIANS POINT OUT THAT WHILE THE EVENTS DEPICTED ARE REAL, THE SHOW EMPHASIZES HAMILTON'S ABOLITIONIST CRED TO AN UNREALISTIC DEGREE. HAMILTON WAS AN ABOLITIONIST, BUT HIS PRIORITIES LAY IN CREATING A NATIONAL BANK AND ENSURING THAT A STRONG RULING CLASS SUPPORTED THE GOVERNMENT. HE EVEN ADVOCATED FOR THE PRESIDENCY TO BE A LIFELONG JOB. THE MUSICAL POKES FUN AT THOMAS JEFFERSON FOR OWNING SLAVES, BUT IT DOESN'T MENTION THAT HAMILTON'S IN-LAWS, THE SCHUYLERS, WERE SLAVEHOLDERS, TOO.

PHILLIPA SOO PLAYED ELIZA SCHUYLER HAMILTON IN THE ORIGINAL PRODUCTION OF THE MUSICAL.

WHILE HAMILTON WAS HARDLY A VILLAIN, HE WAS LIKELY NOT THE MODERN MAN THAT HE SEEMS TO BE IN MIRANDA'S PORTRAYAL EITHER. HE WAS A PRODUCT OF HIS TIMES, AND HIS TRUTH LIES SOMEWHERE IN BETWEEN.

A VICTOR'S SPOILS

3

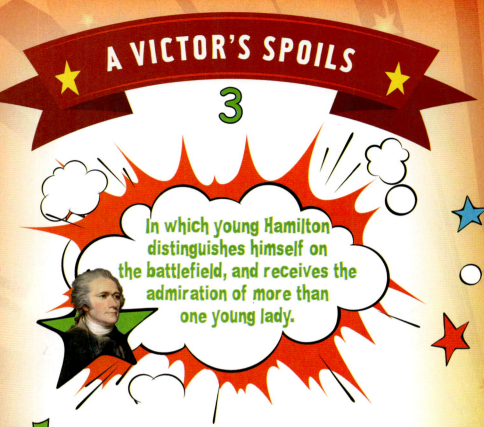

In which young Hamilton distinguishes himself on the battlefield, and receives the admiration of more than one young lady.

Hamilton's military career began with a bang—and not in a good way. About a week after the adoption of the Declaration of Independence, the young captain got his chance to pit his artillery company against two British ships. It was his first foray into battle leadership. But one of the company cannons exploded, killing or wounding several of the men, and the British ships escaped unharmed.

The mishap did not dull Hamilton's eagerness for action.

1776
DECLARATION
OF
INDEPENDENCE

1777
BECAME
AIDE-DE-CAMP
TO GEORGE
WASHINGTON

A 19TH-CENTURY ENGRAVING DEPICTS ALEXANDER HAMILTON AS AN ARTILLERY OFFICER AT THE BATTLE OF YORKTOWN.

1780
MARRIED
ELIZABETH
SCHUYLER

1781
GAINED
FAME AT BATTLE
OF YORKTOWN

45

For about a year, he had juggled academic studies with military training. In fact, his determination to learn on his own the tactical and practical skills needed to wage war was the reason he'd been recommended for an officer's position in the first place. With the need to fight growing more urgent, he had quit his schoolwork to focus full time on the task at hand. War made heroes, and he was consumed with his reputation. But though he might have wished otherwise, the glory of his martial successes would pale before less bloody—but equally crucial—duties.

The British attack on New York was a depressing beginning for the new nation. The city, already a hub of New World financial activity, fell by mid-September. Backed by forces made up of German mercenaries called Hessians, the redcoats easily advanced through Brooklyn and into Manhattan. Though General Washington and his troops were forced to retreat to New Jersey, Hamilton's bravery impressed the general.

That Christmas, Washington commanded one of the most famous maneuvers of the war: the crossing of the icy Delaware River to attack the Hessians camped in Trenton, New Jersey. With 2,400 American troops and 18 pieces of artillery, Washington swarmed the post, killing or wounding about 100 and capturing 900, with minimal American casualties. Hamilton was one of the officers responsible for directing the cannon fire, which was doubly important because it both prevented the enemy from forming ranks (clearing the way for the American infantry) and blocked their escape routes. The victory was an important psychological turning point after a long run of losses. Hamilton's steady performance

AN ENGRAVING IMAGINES THE FIRST MEETING OF GEORGE WASHINGTON (LEFT) AND ALEXANDER HAMILTON.

at Trenton—even more noteworthy because he was ill for much of that winter—and at another battle in nearby Princeton marked him for a quick rise through the ranks.

That rise occurred soon enough, if not in the way the eager-for-the-fight Hamilton likely imagined it would. Within weeks, he was summoned to army headquarters to join General Washington's staff. In March 1777, Hamilton wrote to the Convention of the Representatives of the State of New-York to tell them, "His

Excellency has been pleased to appoint me one of his Aid du Camps," and to advise that they would have to find someone else to lead his company.

Hamilton had mixed feelings about accepting. Being the general's right-hand man and a lieutenant colonel would significantly raise his social cachet. But he remained tempted by the respect that could be won only in the field.

Nonetheless, Hamilton spent much of the rest of the war as Washington's trusted assistant. And it was from that position that he embarked on the path that would assure his place in history. "We tend to look for field commands and battle valor when we're talking about military contributions," says Philip Mead, a curator at the Museum of the American Revolution in Philadelphia, Pennsylvania, "but when Washington and his aides were trying to create a functioning national army, they were accomplishing an extraordinary task in that they were also creating the first American national institution of any real size."

Hamilton was instrumental in that task, with contributions that ranged from crafting new rules for the troops—for example, barring off-duty detachments from undressing at night when the enemy was nearby—to drafting correspondence to French allies. Though he continued to seek opportunities to fight, it was from behind a desk that Hamilton shone.

Working so closely with Washington, Hamilton met many people who would otherwise have been out of his reach. Some were well-positioned men who would become confidants, including a

Turning Water into Wealth

Paterson, New Jersey, is home to the Great Falls, a 77-foot-high waterfall that is the second largest east of the Mississippi River. Hamilton, who once lived in nearby Elizabethtown, knew the spot at the bend of the Passaic River. During a break from the war to have a "modest repast" of tongue, cold ham, and biscuits in July 1778, he showed it off to Washington, fellow aide-de-camp James McHenry, and French officer the marquis de Lafayette. He understood the power-generating potential of the 2 billion gallons that tumbled over the falls each day. In 1791, he chartered the Society for Establishing Useful Manufactures (S.U.M.) with financier William Duer and others. In its prospectus, the society noted that America could not "possess much *active* wealth but as the result of extensive manufactures." The organizers started S.U.M. with $500,000 and named the nation's first planned industrial city in honor of New Jersey governor William Paterson. Pierre Charles L'Enfant, the designer of Washington, D.C., was tapped to figure out how to divert water from the falls, but his too-grand scheme was dismissed. His replacement, Peter Colt, dammed the ravine, formed a reservoir, and created a path along which water could turn a mill. By 1794, the first cotton textile mill was up and running, and the city—and the nation—was in business.

GREAT FALLS, PATERSON, NEW JERSEY

Stumbling on a Traitor

BENEDICT ARNOLD (SEATED) AND MAJOR JOHN ANDRÉ CONSPIRED TO TURN THE FORT AT WEST POINT OVER TO THE BRITISH.

In early fall 1780, George Washington and a group of aides that included Hamilton headed to the fort at West Point, New York, to perform an inspection. They had no reason to suspect that Major General Benedict Arnold, the new commander of the post, would be anything less than a gracious host. But the brash war hero—he had helped take Fort Ticonderoga and had led troops in the Battles of Lake Champlain and Saratoga—had recently been passed over for a promotion. Worse, his lavish lifestyle had left him desperately short of money. So Arnold had secretly sold his allegiance to the British: in return for £20,000 (equivalent to about $3.5 million today) and a high-level army commission, he passed along information about American troop movements and promised to turn over the fort. As Hamilton and James McHenry waited for Washington at Arnold's headquarters a few miles from the fort, word came that Arnold's co-conspirator, British Major John André, had been captured, and maps of West Point had been found in his boot. A flustered Arnold ran upstairs to his wife, Peggy Shippen Arnold, and when Washington showed up, he and the others were left to wonder where Arnold had gone. Eventually, Washington left to inspect the fort, while Hamilton stayed behind. As he sorted through some papers, he heard cries from upstairs. He found Peggy there, seemingly unhinged, holding her baby and talking incoherently. It was a convincing charade, meant to disguise her complicity in her husband's crime. Meanwhile, Arnold had fled and was already on a British sloop of war appropriately christened *Vulture*. When Arnold's betrayal was made clear, Washington asked, "Whom can we trust now?" To Hamilton, Arnold's actions were nothing less than "the blackest treason."

wealthy general named Philip Schuyler. While on a mission for Washington in Albany, New York, in 1777, Hamilton also met General Schuyler's daughter Elizabeth.

As a young lieutenant colonel, Hamilton was known as a ladies' man. It was a reputation fairly earned. He made several romantic attachments to society women he had met because of his military position; in one of the many amorous notes sent to one sweetheart, Kitty Livingston, he wrote, "ALL FOR LOVE is my motto."

But he eventually settled on Elizabeth Schuyler. In the winter of 1779, they became better acquainted at Washington's winter headquarters in Morristown, New Jersey. Elizabeth, sometimes called "Eliza" or "Betsy," was 22 years old. The 25-year-old Hamilton was taken not only with Eliza, but with her entire family as well, especially her sister Angelica. The fascination went both ways, and Hamilton and Angelica conducted

ANGELICA SCHUYLER

an extremely affectionate correspondence until his death. But Angelica was married, so it was to Eliza that Hamilton professed his love. Writing to another Schuyler sister during the courtship, Hamilton said he thought Eliza "most unmercifully handsome," with "good nature, affability, and vivacity." She was considered a great beauty. She was also tougher than many of her peers, making her worthy of the challenges she would face as Mrs. Alexander Hamilton.

The two were married on December 14, 1780, in a small ceremony at the Schuyler mansion. Hamilton, having taken leave from the war for the occasion, returned to service the next month. Eliza soon joined him at headquarters, which were now in New Windsor, New York. There, she became close with Martha Washington, whom she felt was the pinnacle of womanhood.

The fatherless Hamilton was equally attached to General Washington, and might have seen him as more than a boss, especially since Washington referred to his staff as family. That is, until an otherwise unremarkable morning in February 1781, when the two had a falling-out. Passing Hamilton on the stairs, Washington asked for his attention; Hamilton responded with the 18th-century equivalent of "be there in a second" and then continued on his errand, which he described later in a letter to General Schuyler as urgent. On his way back to Washington, he ran into the marquis de Lafayette, who waylaid him with an issue of his own. By the time Hamilton returned, his commander was not pleased. "'Col Hamilton (said he), you have kept me waiting at the head of the stairs these ten minutes,'" the younger man reported in the letter, before adding that the minutes passed were more like two. So when Washington said he felt disrespected, Hamilton responded—respectfully—that if he was serious, then that was that; Hamilton could not work for a man who thought him capable of such a dishonorable act. "I am no longer a member of the General's family," his letter declared.

Some suspect Hamilton had been waiting for an excuse to quit. To his father-in-law, he acknowledged disliking his position of "personal dependence," even to a man he so admired. Plus leaving Washington's staff could mean the possibility of returning to the battlefield. But it was equally possible Hamilton thought the scolding left him no choice. Insults to his character were no small matter for the man who had brought himself up from one of the lowest positions in the colonies.

INSULTS TO HIS CHARACTER WERE NO SMALL MATTER FOR THE MAN WHO HAD BROUGHT HIMSELF UP FROM ONE OF THE LOWEST POSITIONS IN THE COLONIES.

Following the confrontation, Hamilton quickly put aside any potential awkwardness and began to lobby for a battlefield assignment. In petitioning Washington directly, he pointed out that had he never joined the general's staff, he "ought in justice to have been more advanced in rank" than he currently was. That July, Washington put Hamilton in charge of a light-infantry battalion from New York.

The commission came just in time. The war's momentum had turned. France was fighting on America's side, and the progress of the British on most northerly fronts was stalled. A concentrated effort in the South was proving largely futile as well. Within a day of Hamilton's receiving his command, Britain's General Charles Cornwallis led his troops to Yorktown, Virginia, a town on the deep harbor carved by the York River. The decision was a fateful one. Cornwallis was counting on support from the sea, but his

British ships were headed off by the French before they reached the Chesapeake Bay. In the meantime, while decoying the British into thinking New York was their target, Washington's troops and their French allies made their way toward Yorktown. As the summer waned, the British found themselves surrounded by about twice as many Continental Army soldiers. Hamilton was among them.

The Battle of Yorktown commenced at the end of September. The British had encircled their position with defensive shelters, but human reinforcements were far away. The Continental Army began to dig siege lines that allowed soldiers to move cannons closer and closer to Cornwallis's troops. On October 12, Hamilton wrote to his wife, "Thank heaven, our affairs seem to be approaching fast to a happy period." He figured that within five days, the British would surrender or flee; if they did the latter, he predicted only ten more days to finish them off.

Hamilton's analysis was right on. He appealed to Washington again—this time he wanted to lead an attack on one of the fortifications standing in the way of victory. On October 14, Hamilton and his men rushed the position closest to the water. Clambering over the walls, they found themselves face-to-face with the British. Within minutes, the structure was theirs. Soon after, the other fortifications fell, too.

Cornwallis formally surrendered on October 19. America's decisive victory at Yorktown announced that the American army had become a force to fear. As Hamilton wrote to Lafayette, the "rapidity and immediate success of the assault are the best comment on the behaviour of the troops."

A treaty would not be signed until 1783, but the war was essentially over. And though it wasn't his last military action—he helped President Washington end the anti-tax Whiskey Rebellion in 1794, for example—Hamilton's career as a soldier was essentially over, too. He had accomplished all he meant to and more, with spoils that included a commander's respect, access to the most powerful people in the land, a wife—and, not least, a new country to call his own.

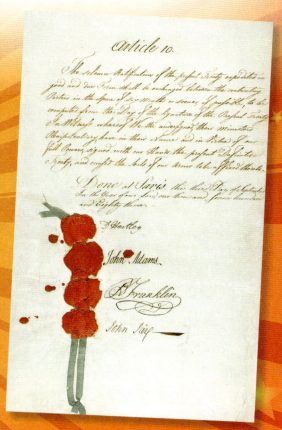

THE TREATY OF PARIS BROUGHT AN OFFICIAL CLOSE TO THE REVOLUTIONARY WAR. IT CARRIES THREE SIGNATURES ON BEHALF OF THE UNITED STATES: JOHN ADAMS, BENJAMIN FRANKLIN, AND JOHN JAY.

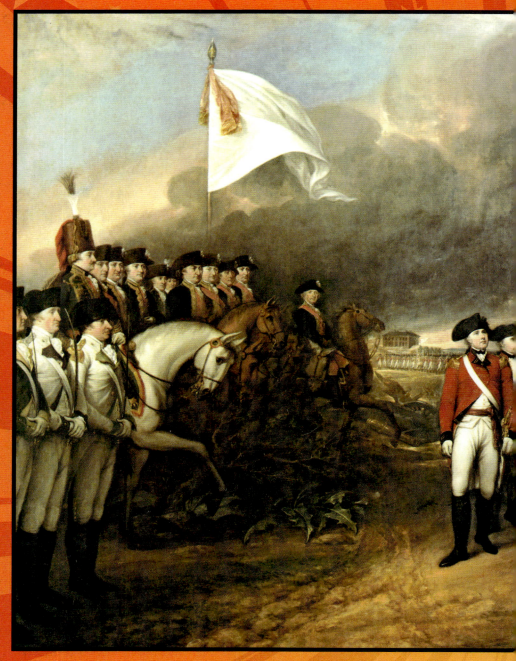

THE SURRENDER OF LORD CORNWALLIS DEPICTS THE MOMENT ON OCTOBER 19, 1781, WHEN BRITISH TROOPS SURRENDERED TO AMERICAN FORCES. LORD CORNWALLIS DID NOT ATTEND THE CEREMONY,

SO GEORGE WASHINGTON (ON THE BROWN HORSE AT RIGHT) DID NOT RIDE FORWARD TO MEET THE BRITISH OFFICERS.

"We Cannot Fail to Be Always Happy."

ALEXANDER HAMILTON AND ELIZABETH SPENT TWO DECADES TOGETHER THROUGH WARTIME TURBULENCE, THE BIRTHS OF EIGHT CHILDREN, SCANDAL, AND THE TRAGIC LOSS OF A FIRSTBORN SON. THROUGH IT ALL, THEY REGARDED EACH OTHER AS SOUL MATES.

THE PORTRAITIST RALPH EARL PAINTED ELIZABETH HAMILTON IN 1787, HIGHLIGHTING HER STRIKING DARK EYES.

MARRYING INTO A PROMINENT NEW YORK FAMILY HELPED HAMILTON'S POSTWAR ADVANCEMENT—AS A LAWYER, TREASURY SECRETARY, AND INSPECTOR GENERAL OF THE ARMY. THEN AGAIN, MARRYING AN UP-AND-COMER HAD SIMILAR PERKS FOR ELIZA.

ELIZABETH'S FATHER, GENERAL PHILIP SCHUYLER, BECAME A CONFIDANT TO HAMILTON.

HAMILTON CALLED HIS WIFE "MY CHARMER" AND "MY ANGEL," AND WHEN THEY WERE APART, HE WAS EAGER TO REUNITE. "HAPPY, HOWEVER I CANNOT BE, ABSENT FROM YOU AND MY DARLING LITTLE ONES," HE WROTE IN 1786, AFTER THE BIRTH OF THEIR THIRD CHILD. "I FEEL THAT NOTHING CAN EVER COMPENSATE FOR THE LOSS OF THE ENJOYMENTS I LEAVE AT HOME. . . . THINK OF ME WITH AS MUCH TENDERNESS AS I DO OF YOU AND WE CANNOT FAIL TO BE ALWAYS HAPPY."

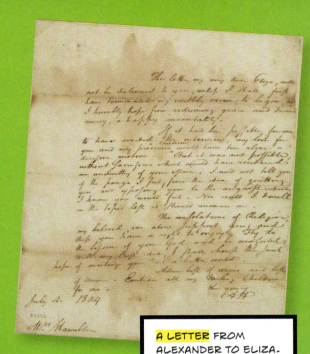

A LETTER FROM ALEXANDER TO ELIZA.

ACCUSED OF IMPROPER FINANCIAL SPECULATION, HAMILTON PUBLISHED A PAMPHLET REVEALING HIS SCANDALOUS AFFAIR WITH MARIA REYNOLDS. ELIZA AND ALEXANDER'S MARRIAGE SURVIVED.

ELIZA LIVED 50 MORE YEARS AFTER ALEXANDER'S DEATH. SHE NEVER REMARRIED, AND DEVOTED HERSELF TO PRESERVING HIS LEGACY.

THOUGH HAMILTON'S RELIGIOUS ZEAL EBBED AND FLOWED, ELIZA WAS A DEVOUT MEMBER OF THE DUTCH REFORMED CHURCH, AND SHE TRUSTED HER HUSBAND'S FAITH. SHE MIGHT NOT HAVE BEEN THE INTELLECT HE WAS, BUT SHE WAS BETTER CONNECTED— BENJAMIN FRANKLIN, FOR ONE, TAUGHT HER HOW TO PLAY BACKGAMMON—AND SHE WAS WELL VERSED IN THE ISSUES OF THE DAY.

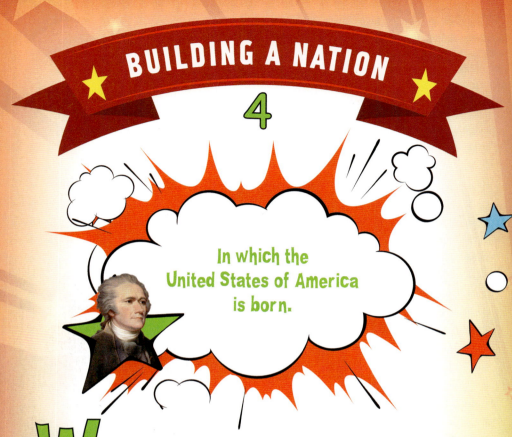

BUILDING A NATION

4

In which the United States of America is born.

With the hard work of the Revolutionary War behind them, Americans now turned to the even harder work of building a new nation. It was easier said than done. Hamilton's experience as Washington's aide had taught him much about economics and international relations, as the American army had suffered greatly from the fact that Britain had forced the colonies to produce only raw materials from the land and to buy more advanced products, like munitions

1782
ADMITTED
TO NEW YORK
STATE BAR

1787
SIGNED
U.S.
CONSTITUTION

PERSUADING 13 INDEPENDENT STATES TO AGREE ON A CODIFIED STATEMENT OF UNITY REQUIRED A SPECIAL MAN. HAMILTON WAS THAT MAN.

1787
STARTED WRITING *THE FEDERALIST* ESSAYS

1789
APPOINTED SECRETARY OF THE TREASURY

and textiles, from the mother country. Not only was fostering a modern economy important for promoting prosperity, it was also a national security imperative.

Equally problematic for the young United States of America was the inflation that these shortages of goods, in combination with the overprinting of paper money, wrought on the economy. Hamilton had an understanding of monetary theory that was impressive considering both his young age and the fact that economics as a field of study didn't even exist as we understand it today. The foundational text of Western economics, Adam Smith's *The Wealth of Nations*, was first published in 1776, the year America declared independence. Through study of such works and his own observations, Hamilton understood that inflation was not just the result of shortages of staple goods and an oversupply of money—it had a psychological component as well.

Even before the war ended, Hamilton saw that the young republic would be crippled by debt if the federal government wasn't given the tools to promote and manage the nation's credit.

The solution to these problems was, in part, the creation of a national banking system that was privately owned but overseen by the federal government through a central bank. As early as 1781, Hamilton was arguing that the power of the British Empire was underwritten not so much by its formidable navy but by a "vast fabric of credit," as he wrote in a letter to Robert Morris, the U.S. superintendent of finance. It was Britain's vigorous financial system, amplified by the deft management of public debt, that enabled the empire to project power farther than any other nation.

Hamilton's correspondence with Morris shows that even during the war, when his days were occupied with the nuts and bolts of the American war effort, he had the mental acuity to continue to master the subjects of international relations and high finance. In his letter to Morris, he argued forcefully for a central bank that could help shoulder the financing of the Revolutionary

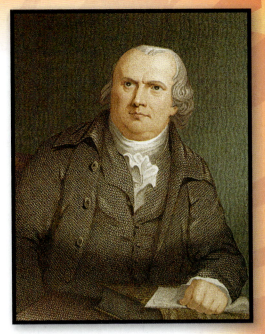

ROBERT MORRIS SUPPORTED HAMILTON'S VISION FOR A NATIONAL BANK.

War effort and turn American sovereign debt from a burden to an advantage. "A national debt if it is not excessive will be to us a national blessing; it will be powerfull cement of our union," Hamilton wrote.

Morris was impressed with the Hamiltonian worldview and was in a position to help carry out these ideas. He successfully petitioned the Continental Congress to establish the Bank of North America to lend money to the fledgling federal government to buy munitions and pay troops. The bank, which the Congress chartered in 1781, was a critical tool in funneling private funds and loans from the French government toward the war effort.

The Bank of North America was an essential institution for helping the states win the Revolutionary War, but the Articles of Confederation that bound the states together did not arrange the right conditions for capitalism and economic growth. Ratified, or approved, that same year, the Articles of Confederation laid out a set of rules by which the nation would be governed. Under the articles, the country was ruled by a congress in which each state had an equal vote and important measures required the consent of at least nine states. But the congress lacked power. It could not regulate trade. It could not impose taxes without the unanimous agreement of all the states. And it could not force states to carry out its directives.

To help right the ship in New York State, local business leaders chose Hamilton to draft the constitution of the Bank of New York, which launched in 1784. The establishment of the bank provided new capital for New York business ventures and smoothed commerce by providing another option, Bank of New York notes, to use as currency.

The Bank of New York brought some degree of order and prosperity to New York City while helping the city gain a few lengths in the race to become America's preeminent commercial city.

But on a wider scale, the United States of America was floundering.

The country fell into an economic depression. Prices, wages, and employment fell. As bankruptcies and foreclosures spread, farmers and small business owners were jammed into prisons for not paying their debts.

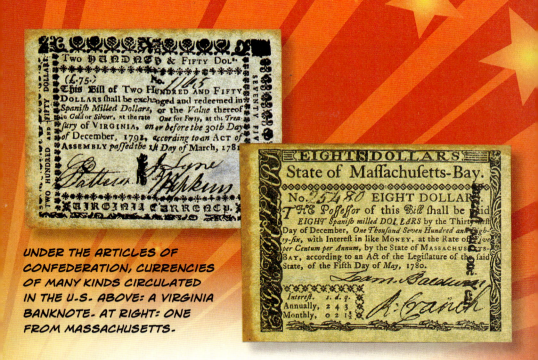

UNDER THE ARTICLES OF CONFEDERATION, CURRENCIES OF MANY KINDS CIRCULATED IN THE U.S. ABOVE: A VIRGINIA BANKNOTE. AT RIGHT: ONE FROM MASSACHUSETTS.

Individual states printed their own money and forced businesses to accept the cash as payment for debts. But the new money quickly lost value. By the spring of 1786, a movement was afoot to change the hopeless Articles of Confederation. But change did not come quickly enough. That autumn, a former militia captain named Daniel Shays started a rebellion in Massachusetts. Armed with guns and pitchforks, angry farmers intimidated judges and shut down courts to prevent the start of bankruptcy proceedings against them.

Representatives from five states met in Annapolis, Maryland, that September to try to settle disputes between the states. They realized that the only way to solve their problems was to amend, or change, the articles. Hamilton, who was attending as the delegate

REPRESENTATIVES FROM FIVE STATES MET AT THE MARYLAND STATE HOUSE.

for the state of New York, wrote a call for each state to send representatives to a meeting in Philadelphia the following May.

The Constitutional Convention of 1787 must have seemed like a dream come true to Hamilton. Presided over by George Washington, the convention was made up of 55 delegates, many of whom were well known throughout the colonies. Though they had been instructed by the Continental Congress to do no more than amend the Articles of Confederation, the delegates set out from the first to produce an entirely new charter of government—the U.S. Constitution. All agreed to keep their debates a secret, although some attendees, including James Madison, kept careful notes that would be published years later.

Hamilton had, by then, been arguing for a stronger national government for nearly a decade. As one of New York's three delegates, he finally had the power to effect change. Or so he thought—his politically cautious New York colleagues consistently outvoted him. Still, he had his say in a grandstanding six-hour speech on June 18, proposing a plan of government so extreme in its centralized authority that it branded him a monarchist.

In the end, delegates John Jay and James Madison sketched out what came to be called the Virginia Plan—a three-part structure of government consisting of an executive, a two-chamber legislature

STATESMAN AND DIPLOMAT JOHN JAY WAS PREVENTED BY ILLNESS FROM CONTRIBUTING MORE EXTENSIVELY. HE WROTE FIVE FEDERALIST ESSAYS.

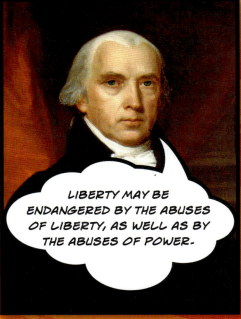

JAMES MADISON LIKELY WROTE 29 OF THE FEDERALIST ESSAYS. HE LATER BECAME A POLITICAL ADVERSARY OF HAMILTON'S.

THE U.S. CONSTITUTION WAS A PRODUCT OF EXTENSIVE DEBATE, DELIBERATION, AND COMPROMISE. THE ORIGINAL DOCUMENT IS HOUSED AT THE NATIONAL ARCHIVES IN WASHINGTON, D.C.

with representation proportional to state population, and a judiciary. Debates on the structure of the legislative branch grew contentious. The smaller states argued against proportional representation, since it would leave them with fewer representatives. In the end, the smaller and larger states compromised. The number of representatives a state could send to the House of Representatives would depend on its population. In the Senate, each state would have an equal number of senators: two.

With that compromise in place, the delegates soon squabbled over how the population of each state would be determined. southern states wanted their large numbers of enslaved people to be counted in their overall populations. Northern states did not want to give the southern states such an advantage in representation. Hamilton, serving as an arbitrator between the delegations, eventually led them to a compromise: for the purpose of the census, each enslaved person would count as three-fifths of a person. In an attempt to balance this concession to slavery, a clause was built into the Constitution that made it possible for the federal government to end the trade of slaves in 1808—but not to free those slaves already traded. The compromises did not sit well with Hamilton, an ardent abolitionist, but he was enough of a pragmatist to believe that it was likely the only way to an agreement.

When the Constitutional Convention drew to a close on September 17, 1787, the delegates had hammered out a system of government that allowed for strong central leadership. Hamilton had successfully advocated for powers like the commerce clause, which gave the federal government the right to coordinate

economic policy across the states, and the necessary and proper clause, which allowed it to take actions necessary for fulfilling its constitutional role.

But before it became the law of the land, the Constitution needed to be ratified by at least nine states. Hamilton invited Madison and Jay to join him in writing a series of newspaper essays defending the proposed Constitution. Publishing under the joint pseudonym Publius, the three wrote 85 essays. Although many were first drafts rushed to press, the collection they were compiled into, *The Federalist* (better known today as *The Federalist Papers*), became a key political text with the launching of the government, and it remains so today. By June of the following year, the Constitution had been ratified by nine states. Two more would sign on soon after.

In April 1789, George Washington journeyed to New York, where the new government would be seated. There, he took the oath of office to become America's first president on April 30, 1789.

Once again, Hamilton's close relationship with Washington would propel his career forward. In September, President Washington made Hamilton secretary of the treasury.

GEORGE WASHINGTON TOOK THE OATH OF OFFICE ON THE BALCONY AT FEDERAL HALL IN NEW YORK.

The Federalist Papers

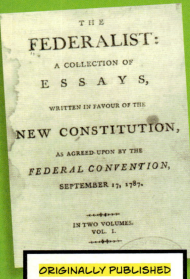

IN THE WEEKS THAT FOLLOWED THE CONSTITUTIONAL CONVENTION, MANY ESSAYS ATTACKING THE NEW DOCUMENT APPEARED IN NEW YORK NEWSPAPERS. CONCERNED ABOUT THE LACK OF REASONED WRITING IN DEFENSE OF THE CONSTITUTION, HAMILTON SOUGHT THE HELP OF SEVERAL OTHER NEW YORK THINKERS. IN THE END, JOHN JAY AND JAMES MADISON AGREED TO PITCH IN. ALL THREE WOULD WRITE UNDER THE SAME PEN NAME: PUBLIUS.

THE FIRST ESSAY, WRITTEN BY HAMILTON, APPEARED IN THE *INDEPENDENT JOURNAL* ON OCTOBER 27, 1787. THE NEXT, WRITTEN BY JAY, APPEARED FOUR DAYS LATER. IN ALL, PUBLIUS WROTE 85 ESSAYS, EACH APPEARING IN ONE OF SEVERAL NEW YORK NEWSPAPERS EVERY FEW DAYS.

THE FEDERALIST PAPERS, AS THEY HAVE COME TO BE KNOWN, WERE A RESOURCE FOR THE STATES AS THEY CONSIDERED WHETHER TO RATIFY. TODAY THEY PROVIDE UNIQUE INSIGHT INTO THE FRAMERS' INTENTIONS IN DRAFTING IT AND ARE AN INVALUABLE TOOL IN INTERPRETING ITS MEANING.

A POLITICAL CARTOON PUBLISHED AFTER NEW HAMPSHIRE RATIFIED THE CONSTITUTION DEPICTS THE STATE OF VIRGINIA RISING TO JOIN THE OTHERS. NEW YORK, WHERE THE *FEDERALIST* ESSAYS WERE PUBLISHED, HAD YET TO JOIN.

"The Federalist No. I"

October 27, 1787

AFTER an unequivocal experience of the inefficacy of the subsisting Fœderal Government, you are called upon to deliberate on a new Constitution for the United States of America. The subject speaks its own importance; comprehending in its consequences, nothing less than the existence of the UNION, the safety and welfare of the parts of which it is composed, the fate of an empire, in many respects, the most interesting the world. It has been frequently remarked, that it seems to have been reserved to the people of this country, by their conduct and example, to decide the important question, whether societies of men are really capable or not, of establishing good government from ref[l]ection and choice, or whether they are forever destined to depend, for their political constitutions, on accident and force. If there be any truth in the remark, the crisis, at which we are arrived, may with propriety be regarded as the æra in which that decision is to be made; and a wrong election of the part we shall act, may, in this view, deserve to be considered as the general misfortune of mankind. . . .

I propose in a series of papers to discuss the following interesting particulars-*The utility of the UNION to your political prosperity— The insufficiency of the present Confederation to preserve that Union—The necessity of a government at least equally energetic with the one proposed to the attainment of this object—The conformity of the proposed constitution to the true principles of republican government—Its analogy to your own state constitution-*and lastly, *The additional security, which its adoption will afford to the preservation of that species of government, to liberty and to property.*

HAMILTON AND MADISON HAD ATTENDED THE CONSTITUTIONAL CONVENTION AND COULD SPEAK TO THE PROCESS THAT CREATED THE DOCUMENT. JAY, WHO WOULD WRITE FIVE FEDERALIST ESSAYS, DID NOT ATTEND.

FEDERALIST NO. 1 LAID OUT THE PREMISE BEHIND THE ESSAYS.

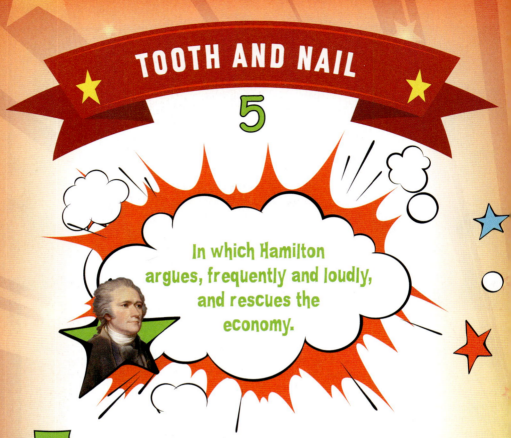

TOOTH AND NAIL

5

In which Hamilton argues, frequently and loudly, and rescues the economy.

Entrusted with bringing order to the nation's chaotic finances, Hamilton had bigger ambitions, taking full advantage of the unstructured new government to advance his policies. Even before the war ended, Hamilton had seen that the young republic would be crippled by debt if the federal government wasn't given the tools to promote and manage the nation's credit. He envisioned a nation fueled by industry, with a strong central government. It would be directed by a strong executive

1790
WROTE
"REPORT ON
PUBLIC CREDIT"

1790
PROPOSED
NATIONAL
BANK

AT THE HELM OF THE NATION'S TREASURY, HAMILTON BEGAN TO REALIZE HIS PLANS FOR STRONG FEDERAL CONTROL OF THE NATION'S BANKS AND CREDIT.

1791
WASHINGTON SIGNED OFF ON NATIONAL BANK PLAN

1791
"REPORT ON MANUFACTURES" WAS REJECTED

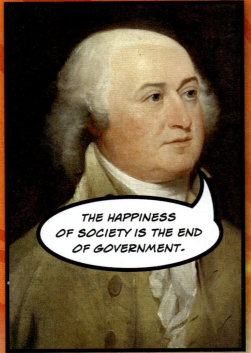

THE HAPPINESS OF SOCIETY IS THE END OF GOVERNMENT.

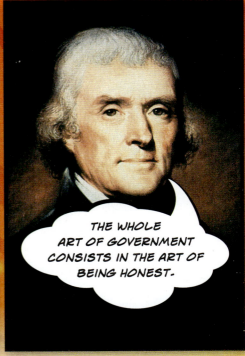

THE WHOLE ART OF GOVERNMENT CONSISTS IN THE ART OF BEING HONEST.

ALTHOUGH HE WAS ALSO A FEDERALIST, JOHN ADAMS WAS WARY OF BANKS. HE WOULD LATER BECOME AN ADVERSARY OF HAMILTON.

SECRETARY OF STATE THOMAS JEFFERSON SHARED MADISON'S FEAR OF "MONARCHICAL" CENTRAL POWER.

and stabilized by the support of the rich and powerful. It was a grand vision, and one that was almost guaranteed to put him at odds with many in the new government.

Some of the most influential Founding Fathers and framers of the Constitution, from Thomas Jefferson to John Adams to James Madison, were deeply suspicious of banks and fought hard to shield the new republic from their influence. Before the Revolutionary War, the states had been overwhelmingly agricultural. A large majority of the delegates to the Constitutional Convention were farmers whose relationships to banks and bankers were adversarial. Many of America's leading statesmen, therefore, were wary of finance and banking. Their philosophy derived in part from personal experience. Jefferson fought his whole life to stay one step ahead of his debt collectors.

Hamilton was nearly alone among the intellectual powerhouses of the early republic in his defense of a vigorous banking system as necessary not only for the economic security of the nation but also for the full flowering of its people. His pedigree as the poor, propertyless son of a single mother offered him another perspective on banking and money and how these tools might be used to bring prosperity to a young nation.

Madison, one of the chief architects of the Constitution, had been elected a U.S. representative for Virginia and also served as an adviser to the president. Like many Americans, wary after finally shaking off the British monarchy, he was opposed to the idea of a strong central government. As time went on, Hamilton and Madison would split bitterly. Madison's equal and ally in those fights was Jefferson, author of the Declaration of Independence and Washington's secretary of state.

In the fall of 1789, Congress had asked Hamilton to propose a scheme to retire America's substantial wartime debt. During the war, states had borrowed money from individuals and foreign nations. Many states still had that debt—and were unable to pay it off. In January 1790, Hamilton came back with a far-reaching "Report Relative to a Provision for the Support of Public Credit."

He proposed that the federal government assume all the debt—about $77 million altogether—and allow debt holders to exchange their old promissory notes for new federal securities. The government would promise to set aside tax revenues each year to cover the new bonds—but no more than 2% of them in any year. That would not only ease the federal payout but also ensure that the securities would circulate and be traded over the years, much like currency.

Both during and after the war, many holders of American debt, doubting their notes would ever be redeemable and hoping to get at least something for them, sold them to speculators at prices well below face value. Hamilton's plan called for full face value to be paid to whoever held the new federal papers, which would richly reward those same speculators. Hamilton was untroubled by that prospect. He hoped some of them would become wealthy enough to develop into lenders themselves, providing capital to spur economic growth.

Hamilton's plan assumed that the government had significant power to guide the economy. Madison would emerge as an increasingly vocal leader of the opposition to Hamilton's scheme. (Jefferson, prevented from speaking publicly by his position in Washington's cabinet, opposed the idea privately.) In February, Madison put before the House a measure that required the

HAMILTON'S PLAN ASSUMED THAT THE GOVERNMENT HAD SIGNIFICANT POWER TO GUIDE THE ECONOMY.

government to make payment of at least some kind to any original holders of debt who had sold to speculators. Hamilton objected that this would be illegal, because the notes said on their faces that they would be payable to the bearers—meaning the current holders, not whoever might have held them earlier. It would also be impossible to track down all the original holders.

Hamilton's arguments prevailed, and Madison's proposed measure was defeated. But in June, when the House agreed to most of Hamilton's funding scheme, it did not approve one of its central elements: his plan to have the federal government assume state-issued debt. States like Virginia, Maryland, and Georgia, which had already repaid most of their wartime debt, objected to "assumption" because it asked them to help pay the obligations of less conscientious states. And anyone determined to rein in federal power recognized that by assuming state debt—and with it the right to collect taxes to repay that debt—the central government would gain additional power at the expense of the states. In fact, that had been one of Hamilton's reasons for proposing the plan.

On June 20, 1790, Hamilton met with Madison and Jefferson over dinner. The two men made him a surprising offer. At the time, the government was embroiled in another debate on a very different subject—the location of a capital city for the country. As Virginians, Jefferson and Madison wanted it to be based on the Potomac River. They promised to help pass Hamilton's assumption bill if Hamilton would agree to lobby northern congressional delegations to support the Potomac site. Hamilton

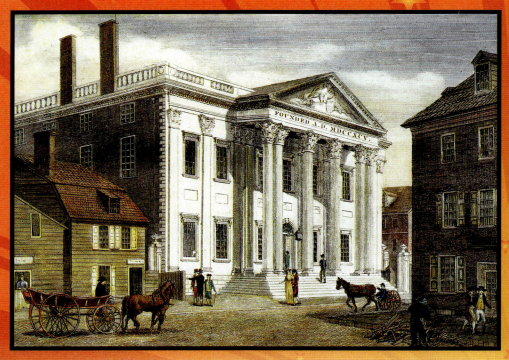

THE BANK OF THE UNITED STATES WAS CONSTRUCTED ON THIRD STREET IN PHILADELPHIA, WHERE IT STILL STANDS TODAY.

badly wanted New York to become the nation's permanent capital, but he wanted the assumption bill more. A few weeks after their dinner, Congress did indeed opt for the location on the Potomac. A month after that, the Funding Act, which included provisions for assumption, passed.

Hamilton wasn't finished yet. In December, he proposed his most radical idea yet—that Congress should charter a national bank. His Bank of the United States would assist in collecting taxes, handle payments on the debt, issue notes that could be used as currency, and make loans to both the government and private businesses.

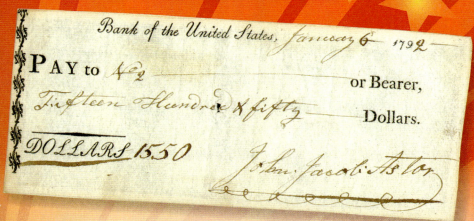

The bank's ownership would be split between private investors and the Treasury Department at a ratio of four to one, with the federal government maintaining the right to oversee the bank's books. The bank was massive for its time: its $10 million in initial capital (roughly $260 million in 2015 dollars) was more than three times as large as the combined capital of the five state-chartered banks. Its large size enabled it to market federal debt across the country and abroad, leading to low and stable interest rates and a sound currency.

The bank was quickly approved by the Senate. But in the House, Madison argued that the Constitution did not give the federal government the power to establish such an institution. When the House approved the bank and sent the bill to the president for his signature, Madison urged Washington to veto it. Attorney General Edmund Randolph sent Washington a memo agreeing that it was unconstitutional. Jefferson backed them up.

The president was largely sympathetic to his young treasury secretary's vision of an economically powerful America. But he decided that if he could not counter the arguments of his advisers, he would veto the bill. Hamilton obliged him with a lengthy written argument in favor of the bank, which was also a brilliant argument for what we now call a "loose construction" of the Constitution. The bank was lawful, he declared, because the clause of the Constitution empowering the government to take all steps "necessary and proper" to execute its enumerated powers gave it "implied powers" to take measures not specifically set out in the text. What Hamilton laid out in his letter was the first clear statement of what would become an enduring and highly influential interpretation of the Constitution. It certainly convinced the president, who signed the bill.

When shares in the bank went on sale for the first time on July 4, they turned out to be more popular than even Hamilton had expected. Investors, most of them in Boston, New York, and Philadelphia, bought up all of them within an hour. Then there followed a months-long wave of speculative fever in connection with the sale of "scrip"—certificates entitling the holders to buy shares at a later date. In the space of a single month, the price for one piece of scrip rose from $25 to $325. The spectacle of "scrippomania" horrified Jefferson, who bemoaned "the rage of getting rich in a day." Even Hamilton worried that the speculative frenzy could harm the system of public credit "by disgusting all sober citizens and giving a wild air to everything."

Hamilton's battle against Jefferson and Madison was far from over. Jefferson and Madison spent part of that summer traveling together in New York State, seeking allies in their fight against Hamilton and the powerful federal government he seemed to be creating. Everywhere he looked, Jefferson saw evidence that Hamilton and his supporters were attempting to steer the young republic toward monarchy. The federal government had moved from New York to Philadelphia, and Jefferson persuaded a well-known poet and journalist, Philip

THE *NATIONAL GAZETTE* BECAME A TIRELESS CRITIC OF HAMILTON'S POLICIES.

Freneau, to move as well. Freneau would start a publication, the *National Gazette*, that could become a platform for attacks on the Hamiltonian vision—and on Hamilton himself. By that means, Jefferson and Madison hoped to shape voter opinion before the next year's congressional elections and help elect representatives supporting a states' rights agenda.

Over the following year, Madison would use the pages of the *Gazette* to publish no fewer than 18 anonymous attacks on Hamilton and his policies.

In December 1791, Hamilton delivered a new report, "on the Subject of Manufactures." He proposed that the government aid businesses through direct subsidies, rewards for inventions, targeted tariffs, and improved roads and river transport. Manufacturing, he expected, would take place largely in the North, with southern states supplying raw materials. Women and children would become part of the factory workforce.

But while President Washington shared his enthusiasm for the growth of manufacturing in America, he considered much of what Hamilton was advocating to be unconstitutional. And anyway, he said, it did not "comport with the temper of the times"—another way of saying the country wasn't ready to be pushed into the industrial future. Congress took no action on Hamilton's plan.

As 1792 opened, the first political parties had begun to solidify. Hamilton and those of his outlook would come to be called Federalists. On the other side were Madison, Jefferson, and their allies, who would gradually coalesce into the Democratic-Republican Party, commonly known as Republicans (not the same as today's Republicans). All through that year, Madison and Jefferson's anti-Hamilton campaign continued, with Hamilton resorting to anonymous journalism in reply and Washington trying in vain to reconcile his squabbling advisers. In May, Jefferson sent Washington a letter accusing Hamilton of sapping the nation's morality by introducing a spirit of gambling and vice, and warning that he wanted to establish a monarchy.

The three managed to agree on only one thing that summer.

When Washington told Madison that he planned to retire at the end of his term, all three begged him to stay in office.

As the elections of 1792 approached, the conflict between Federalists and Republicans intensified. It was in that political moment that Hamilton developed a deep dislike for a politician named Aaron Burr. In 1789, Hamilton's father-in-law, General Philip Schuyler, had become one of New York's first two senators. When Schuyler, a Federalist, ran

PHILIP SCHUYLER

for re-election in 1791, anti-Federalist opponents nominated Burr to replace him. When Burr's campaign succeeded, it made a lifelong enemy of Hamilton: "I fear the other Gentleman [Burr] is unprincipled both as a public and private man. When the constitution was in deliberation, his conduct was equivocal; but its enemies, who I believe best understood him considered him as with them. In fact, I take it, he is for or against nothing, but as it suits his interest or ambition. . . . I feel it a religious duty to oppose his career."

A STATUE OF ALEXANDER HAMILTON IN FRONT OF THE TREASURY BUILDING IN WASHINGTON, D.C., PAYS TRIBUTE TO HIS LEGACY.

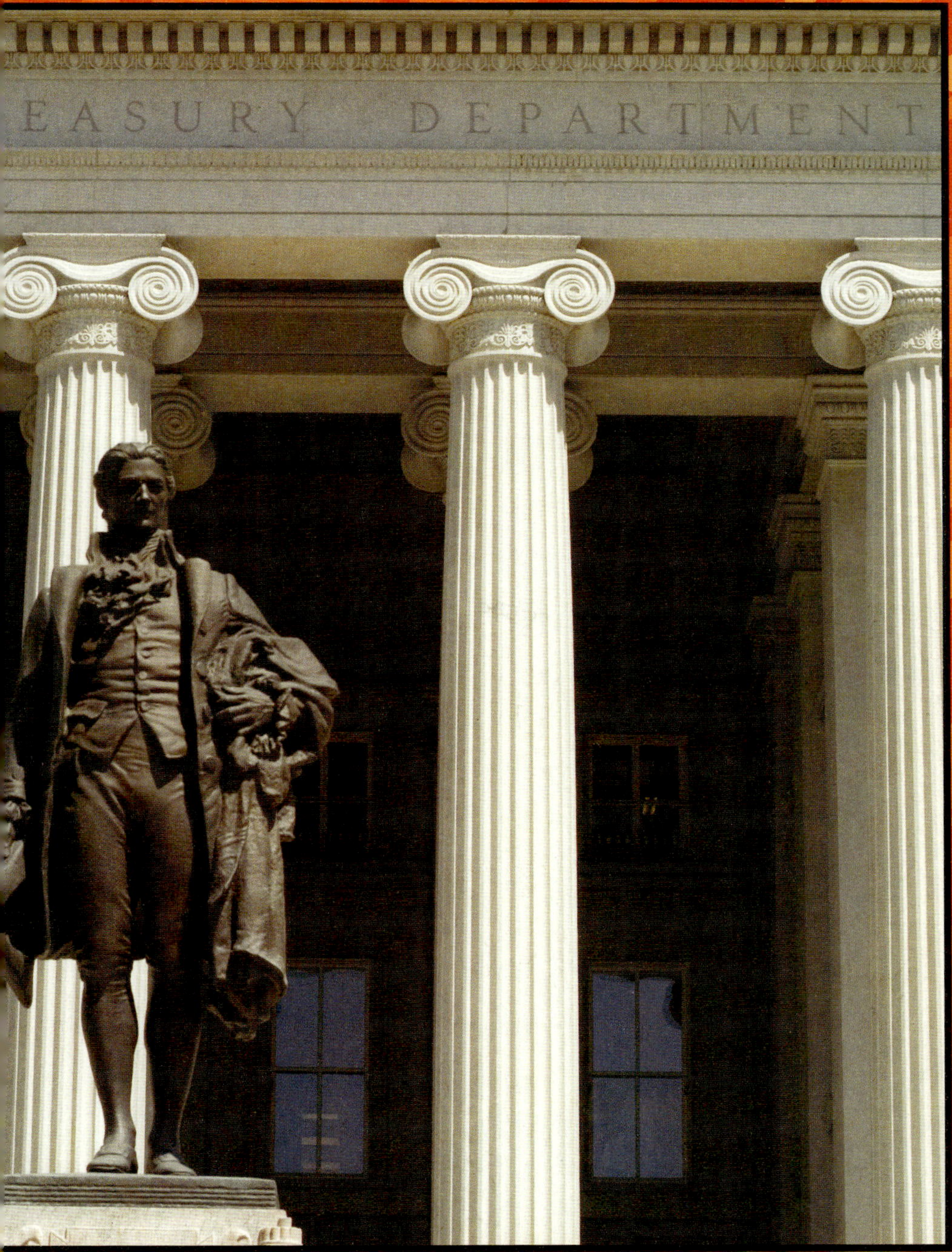
EASURY DEPARTMENT

Face Off: Alexander Hamilton and the $10 Bill

ALEXANDER HAMILTON IS PROBABLY BEST KNOWN BY THE AVERAGE AMERICAN AS THE MAN ON THE $10 BILL, AS HAS BEEN THE CASE FOR GENERATIONS. AS THE NATION'S FIRST TREASURY SECRETARY, HAMILTON WAS A NATURAL CHOICE TO BE FEATURED ON U.S. CURRENCY, AND HE HAS CONSISTENTLY HAD A PLACE ON AMERICAN PAPER MONEY SINCE THE GOVERNMENT BEGAN PRINTING IT DURING THE CIVIL WAR.

FOLLOWING THE AMERICAN REVOLUTION, HAMILTON WAS THE FOUNDING FATHER WHO CHAMPIONED A VIGOROUS FINANCIAL SYSTEM UNDERWRITTEN BY THE FEDERAL GOVERNMENT. HE ADVOCATED FOR THE FEDERAL ASSUMPTION OF STATE DEBTS AFTER THE REVOLUTION, AND HE ARGUED FORCEFULLY FOR THE CREATION OF THE BANK OF THE UNITED STATES—ACTIONS THAT HELPED BIND THE NATION TOGETHER AND ESTABLISH AMERICAN CREDITWORTHINESS ABROAD.

HAMILTON HAS APPEARED ON BILLS SINCE THEY WERE FIRST PRINTED, DURING THE CIVIL WAR. FROM TOP TO BOTTOM: 1861, 1862, 1878, 1882, AND 2006.

IN JUNE 2015, MANY WERE
SHOCKED WHEN THE U.S. TREASURY
ANNOUNCED THAT THE $10 BILL
WOULD BE REDESIGNED TO FEATURE
A WOMAN IN HAMILTON'S PLACE.

THOUGH A FEW WOMEN HAVE
BEEN FEATURED ON U.S. COINS AND
PRECIOUS METAL CERTIFICATES,
THERE HAS NEVER BEEN A WOMAN
ON A WIDELY CIRCULATED FEDERAL
RESERVE NOTE. A GROUP CALLED
WOMEN ON 20S PETITIONED THE
WHITE HOUSE TO REPLACE PRESIDENT
ANDREW JACKSON ON THE $20
BILL WITH A NOTABLE WOMAN FROM
THE COUNTRY'S HISTORY. INSTEAD
OF GIVING JACKSON THE BOOT,
HOWEVER, TREASURY OFFICIALS
DECIDED THAT IT WOULD BE HAMILTON
WHO WOULD GO, BECAUSE THE $10
BILL WAS THE NEXT NOTE UP FOR A
REDESIGN.

IN THE END, IT MIGHT HAVE BEEN
THE MUSICAL *HAMILTON* THAT SAVED
ITS SUBJECT'S PLACE ON THE BILL.
THE MUSICAL INCREASED AWARENESS
OF HAMILTON'S STORY, AND THE
TREASURY ANNOUNCED IN 2016
THAT HE WOULD STAY IN PLACE.

SEVERAL WOMEN WERE PROPOSED AS
REPLACEMENTS FOR HAMILTON ON THE
BILL. FROM TOP TO BOTTOM: AMELIA
EARHART, ROSA PARKS, ELEANOR
ROOSEVELT, AND HARRIET TUBMAN.

THE PORTRAIT OF HAMILTON ON THE CURRENT $10 BILL IS THE ONLY
LEFT-FACING ONE FEATURED ON A FEDERAL RESERVE NOTE, AND HAMILTON
IS ONE OF JUST TWO PEOPLE ON PAPER MONEY WHO NEVER SERVED AS
PRESIDENT. (BENJAMIN FRANKLIN IS THE OTHER.) HAMILTON'S PORTRAIT IS
ALSO NOTABLE BECAUSE IT WAS PAINTED BY THE FAMED AMERICAN ARTIST
JOHN TRUMBULL, KNOWN FOR HIS DEPICTIONS OF SCENES FROM THE
REVOLUTIONARY WAR AND THE EARLY REPUBLIC. HIS MOST FAMOUS WORK
IS *THE DECLARATION OF INDEPENDENCE*, FINISHED IN 1818, WHICH SHOWS
THE SIGNING OF JEFFERSON'S FAMOUS DOCUMENT AND IS FEATURED ON THE
REVERSE SIDE OF THE $2 BILL.

THE LONG FALL

6

In which Hamilton's temper—and his past—catches up with him.

amilton the nationalist was a divisive politician. By 1795, he was also a tired one. With the nation's finances in order and his own finances suffering, he resigned from office and returned to New York to practice law. But even in private life, Hamilton was plagued by slander and scandal.

In the summer of 1791, a woman named Maria (pronounced *mah-RYE-uh*) Reynolds had gone to Hamilton's home in Philadelphia, telling a story of an abusive husband who had run

1791 CAUGHT IN SCANDAL

1795 RESIGNED CABINET POSITION TO PRACTICE LAW

off, leaving her destitute. Hamilton agreed to bring money to her house. When he arrived there, as he later wrote, "Some conversation ensued from which it was quickly apparent that other than pecuniary consolation would be acceptable."

So began what might well be America's first political sex scandal. Hamilton's attachment to Maria lasted at least a year, even after her husband, James, began blackmailing Hamilton—$1,000 in exchange for his silence. Hamilton began to pay in installments, and he tried more than once to end the relationship, but each time either Maria or James would claim she was grief-stricken

A LARGER-THAN-LIFE STATUE OF HAMILTON CAN BE FOUND IN NEW YORK'S CENTRAL PARK.

and had to see him again. The entreaties have raised the question of whether the affair was devised as a trap from the start. Making matters worse, a political foe, Jacob Clingman, saw Hamilton leaving the Reynolds home more than once. When confronted, Maria told him that Hamilton had been involved with her husband in some improper financial speculation.

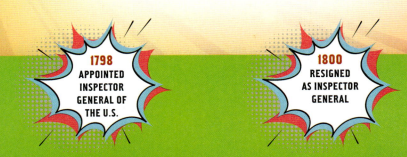

1798
APPOINTED INSPECTOR GENERAL OF THE U.S.

1800
RESIGNED AS INSPECTOR GENERAL

Hamilton finally disentangled himself from the couple, making his last payment in June 1792. But rumors that he was covering up illegal speculation persisted. When Clingman brought letters implying just that to other politicians, they confronted Hamilton. Eager to prove he had not compromised his role as treasury secretary, he confessed to his private misdeeds. But though he asked the group to keep the truth secret, it eventually leaked. Some suspect the clerk who had copied Clingman's notes for Monroe. In 1797, a crude pamphleteer named James Thomson Callender publicly charged Hamilton with inappropriate behavior.

Hamilton had been accused of infidelity in print before, and his enduring reputation as a flirt made it easy to believe he had transgressed again. (In truth, there is no proof of his straying any other time in his marriage.) Furious that his public record was being besmirched, he went on the offensive. Freed from the confines of his government post and no longer reporting to Washington, he responded by running wild in print. He countered the charges by confessing in a shocking tell-all pamphlet that stunned friends and enemies alike.

"The charge against me is a connection with one James Reynolds for the purposes of improper pecuniary speculation," he wrote in the 95-page booklet. "My real crime is an amorous connection with his wife, for a considerable time with his privity and connivance, if not originally brought on by a combination between the husband and wife with the design to extort money from me."

Revealing the details of the dalliance struck many as excessive, and his wife must have been devastated by the attention. Hamilton acknowledged as much in his booklet: "I can never cease to condemn myself for the pang, which [this confession] may inflict in a bosom eminently intitled to all my gratitude, fidelity and love."

Eliza was pregnant when the infidelity became public, and Hamilton held off on publishing his response until after she delivered their sixth child. For her part, Eliza never publicly commented on the scandal, and her husband's notes to her were still as sweet as ever. "I always feel how necessary you are to me," he wrote in 1798. "But when you are absent I become still more sensible of it, and look around in vain for that satisfaction which you alone can bestow."

Two years later, in 1800, Hamilton stumbled again. Still eager to steer national policy, he had secretly advised members of President John Adams's cabinet for years. When Adams found out, he flew into a rage, forcing out Hamilton's supporters and denouncing him as a "Creole bastard" leading a British faction. Hamilton responded with a 54-page pamphlet that savaged Adams's character. But his effort to replace Adams with a more pliable candidate in the pending election instead divided his party, throwing victory to the Republicans. Condemned as "radically deficient in discretion" by his fellow Federalists, Hamilton fell from power.

CONDEMNED AS "RADICALLY DEFICIENT IN DISCRETION" BY HIS FELLOW FEDERALISTS, HAMILTON FELL FROM POWER.

Hamilton's House

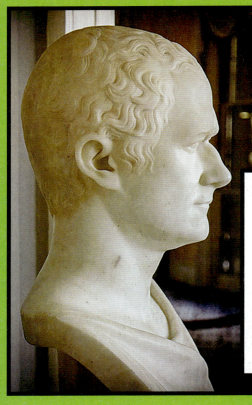

HAMILTON SPENT HIS FIRST 29 YEARS IN NEW YORK MOVING FROM HOUSE TO HOUSE IN LOWER MANHATTAN, OWNING NONE OF THEM. IT WASN'T UNTIL THE LATE 1790S, HIS CAREER IN PUBLIC SERVICE MOSTLY THROUGH, THAT HAMILTON DECIDED TO BUILD A TRANQUIL RETREAT.

HAMILTON WAS FLATTERED WHEN ITALIAN SCULPTOR GIUSEPPE CERACCHI APPROACHED HIM ABOUT PRODUCING A BUST, AND HE WAS HAPPY TO SIT WHILE CERACCHI MODELED THE CAST. BUT WHEN THE SCULPTOR RETURNED FROM ITALY WITH THE MARBLE BUST, HE PRESENTED HAMILTON WITH AN UNEXPECTED BILL OF $620 (ABOUT $15,000 TODAY). HAMILTON EVENTUALLY PAID UP. AS IT TURNS OUT, CERACCHI PULLED THE SAME SCAM ON WASHINGTON AND JEFFERSON.

BEING A FOUNDING FATHER DID NOT PAY PARTICULARLY WELL, AND HAMILTON, TOO PROUD TO ACCEPT MONEY FROM HIS IN-LAWS, HAD STRETCHED HIS CREDIT TO THE LIMIT. WHILE RENTING A SMALL HOUSE IN HARLEM HEIGHTS, IN WHAT WAS ESSENTIALLY THE COUNTRYSIDE OF NORTHERN MANHATTAN, HE FOUND THE BEST PLOT OF LAND HE COULD AFFORD: 15 ACRES, PERCHED HIGH ENOUGH ON A HILL TO OFFER VIEWS OF MANHATTAN'S TWO BORDERING RIVERS. HE WAS SO TAKEN BY THE SPOT THAT HE SOON BOUGHT 20 ACRES MORE. FROM THERE, IT WAS AN HOUR-AND-A-HALF COMMUTE BY CARRIAGE TO HIS LAW OFFICES AT THE OTHER END OF THE ISLAND.

HAMILTON CHOSE JOHN MCCOMB, JR.—WHO HAD DESIGNED GRACIE MANSION, AND WOULD LATER DESIGN NEW YORK'S CITY HALL—TO ARCHITECT HIS DREAM HOUSE.

IN 1802, THE RESIDENCE WAS COMPLETED, IN THE FEDERAL ARCHITECTURAL STYLE. HAMILTON NAMED IT THE GRANGE, AFTER BOTH HIS UNCLE'S ST. CROIX PLANTATION AND HIS GRANDFATHER'S ESTATE IN SCOTLAND.

THE GRANGE AT ITS FIRST ADDRESS.

IN THE END, HAMILTON WAS ABLE TO ENJOY THE GRANGE FOR ONLY TWO YEARS. AFTER HIS FATAL DUEL IN 1804, HIS BELOVED ELIZA WAS LEFT WITH HER HUSBAND'S DEBTS BUT NOT THE HOUSE, WHICH WAS SOLD AT AUCTION. BUT, USING THE INHERITANCE SHE RECEIVED FROM HER FATHER AND SOME DONATIONS FROM GENEROUS FRIENDS, SHE SOON BOUGHT IT BACK. AND SHE WOULD LIVE AT THE GRANGE FOR NEARLY THREE MORE DECADES, UNTIL SHE SOLD IT AND MOVED TO WASHINGTON, D.C., IN 1833.

IN 1889, THE HOUSE WAS SET TO BE DEMOLISHED. JUST BEFORE THE GRANGE WAS LOST FOREVER, ITS OWNER, AMOS COTTING, DONATED IT TO ST. LUKE'S EPISCOPAL CHURCH. THE CHURCH BROUGHT IN A CONSTRUCTION FIRM TO LIFT THE GRANGE OFF ITS FOUNDATION, AND THE HOUSE—MINUS A PORCH OR TWO—WAS DRAWN BY HORSES TO CONVENT AVENUE, 500 FEET AWAY. WHEN A NEW CHURCH BUILDING WAS ERECTED, THE HOUSE WAS WEDGED BESIDE IT AND TURNED INTO A RECTORY.

FOR ALMOST 120 YEARS, THE GRANGE SAT WEDGED AGAINST ST. LUKE'S CHURCH ON CONVENT AVENUE.

IN 2008, THE HOUSE WAS MOVED ONE MORE TIME, FROM CONVENT AVENUE TO ST. NICHOLAS PARK. AFTER TWO YEARS OF WORK— A REMADE ROOF, A REWIRED ELECTRICAL SYSTEM, REAPPOINTED ERA-SPECIFIC DECORATIVE TOUCHES—HAMILTON GRANGE NATIONAL MEMORIAL OPENED ITS DOORS AS A MUSEUM IN 2011. ITS PRESENT SITE OVERLAPS THE LAND ITS FIRST OWNER ONCE BOUGHT.

IN 2008, THE GRANGE WAS LIFTED OFF ITS FOUNDATION AND ROLLED AROUND THE CORNER TO ST. NICHOLAS PARK.

ABOVE: A RESTORED HAMILTON GRANGE NATIONAL MEMORIAL WELCOMES VISITORS NOT FAR FROM WHERE IT ORIGINALLY STOOD. RIGHT: THE DINING ROOM.

THE TWO-STORY BUILDING FEATURED NOT ONE BUT TWO OCTAGONAL ROOMS, ONE OF THEM A DINING ROOM WITH TALL FRENCH WINDOWS. WHEN THE CONNECTING DOORS TO THE PARLOR WERE OPEN, THE COMBINED SPACE PROVIDED AN EXPANSIVE AND ELEGANT ROOM FOR ENTERTAINING. A SMALL STUDY OFF THE FOYER FEATURED BOOKSHELVES AND HELD A ROLLING DESK WHERE HAMILTON WROTE HIS LETTERS. OUTSIDE, LARGE PORCHES AND VERANDAS PROVIDED PLENTY OF OUTDOOR SPACE, AND A ROW OF 13 SWEET GUM TREES NEAR THE ENTRANCE PAID HOMAGE TO THE ORIGINAL COLONIES.

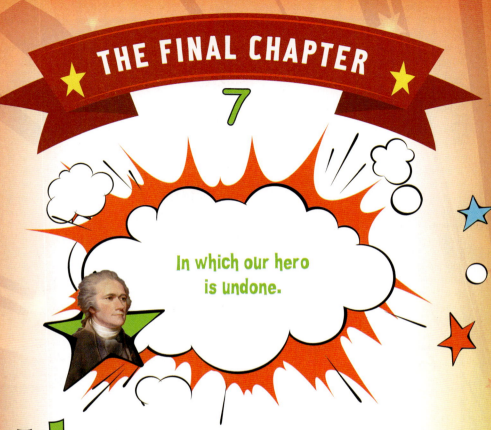

In which our hero
is undone.

Until the passage of the 12th Amendment to the Constitution, presidential elections were not decided by popular vote, but rather by electors appointed by each state's legislature. The candidate with the most votes became president, and the runner-up was vice president. In designing this system, the framers had assumed that the electors would cast their votes for candidates based on their individual merits. But with the rise of the party system, the electors began swearing to vote for

1801
JEFFERSON
AND BURR TIED
FOR PRESIDENT

1801
HELPED FOUND
THE *NEW-YORK
EVENING POST*

the candidates in particular parties. This meant that electoral votes could easily be equally split between two candidates from the same party. In 1801, in part as a result of Hamilton's ill-fated meddling, Aaron Burr and Thomas Jefferson tied with 73 votes each, sending the decision to the House of Representatives, where voting resulted in 35 more deadlocks.

While Hamilton opposed Jefferson's ideas, he disliked Burr even more. He lobbied many

THE RULE OF MY LIFE IS TO MAKE BUSINESS A PLEASURE, AND PLEASURE MY BUSINESS.

AARON BURR

influencers, including Oliver Wolcott, Jr.—his successor as secretary of the treasury—to ensure that Burr would be denied the presidency. He wrote to Wolcott, "There is no doubt but that upon every virtuous and prudent calculation Jefferson is to be preferred. He is by far not so dangerous a man and he has pretensions to character.

1801
PHILIP HAMILTON KILLED IN A DUEL

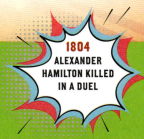

1804
ALEXANDER HAMILTON KILLED IN A DUEL

"As to *Burr* there is nothing in his favour. His private character is not defended by his most partial friends. He is bankrupt beyond redemption except by the plunder of his country. His public principles have no other spring or aim than his own aggrandisement."

On the 36th vote, Jefferson and Hamilton got what they wanted. Thomas Jefferson would be president. And Aaron Burr, vice president.

THE TALENTS AND TRAITS THAT HAD RAISED HAMILTON TO PROMINENCE HAD DESTROYED HIM.

The talents and traits that had raised Hamilton to prominence—voracious ambition, compulsive self-expression, bold self-assertion—had destroyed him, and helped lift his political foe. But Hamilton was not one to stay silent. In 1801, he helped launch a newspaper. In its first edition, on November 16, the *New-York Evening Post* (which still exists today as the *New York Post*) promised to print only worthy stories: "The design of this paper is to diffuse among the people correct information on all interesting subjects, to inculcate just principles in religion, morals, and politics, and to cultivate a taste for sound literature." In reality, though, the newspaper was zealously committed to advancing the views of the Federalist Party at the expense of the Democratic-Republicans, the party of President Thomas Jefferson. Hamilton, a prolific writer, would contribute only one bylined piece to the *Evening Post*—a rebuttal to a report that at the Battle of Yorktown during the Revolutionary War, the marquis de Lafayette had ordered Hamilton to execute British prisoners. But he authored 18 pro-Federalist pieces under the pen name Lucius Crassus, all of them vigorous attacks on Jefferson.

Hamilton had conceived the enterprise with a group of staunch political allies who loathed the anti-Federalist climate in both New York State and Washington, D.C. Each of the founders was asked to invest at least $100; for his part, Hamilton might have pitched in as much as $1,000. Early readers, including such illustrious New Yorkers as merchant John Jacob Astor and banker Anthony Bleecker, paid a hefty $8 for a yearly subscription; the paper was not sold to the rabble in the streets.

The *Evening Post* was only a week old when it was forced to cover one of the most tragic events of Hamilton's life: the death of his beloved son Philip in a duel with a 27-year-old lawyer and Jefferson supporter, George Eacker. According to Ron Chernow's biography of Hamilton, his father had counseled Philip to either shoot into the air or avoid firing altogether, so that if he were killed, it would be viewed as a homicide. And that's how the paper depicted the event: as Eacker having "murdered" the 19-year-old man (while neglecting to mention that Philip had fired, too).

Hamilton never fully recovered after his son's death. But his political principles never wavered, nor did his habit of saying more than he should.

In 1804, when Aaron Burr ran for governor of New York, Hamilton plunged back into politics to oppose him. Confronted by written evidence of Hamilton's invective, Burr initiated an affair of

The Hamiltons

Alexander and Elizabeth Schuyler Hamilton had eight children:

Philip The eldest Hamilton was named after his grandfather, Revolutionary War general Philip Schuyler. In 1801, he got into an argument with George Eacker at the Park Theater in New York City and was fatally wounded in the subsequent duel—not far from the spot in New Jersey where his father would fall three years later.

Angelica Her brother's death caused her to have a nervous breakdown, and though her father tried to perk her up with gifts of parakeets and watermelons, she never improved. She was an invalid until her death at 72.

Alexander Born in May 1786, he graduated from Columbia College. He learned British military tactics in the Duke of Wellington's army in Portugal, and then served as a U.S. captain in the War of 1812. He became a U.S. district attorney in New York.

James Alexander He was a major in the War of 1812, was briefly acting secretary of state under President Andrew Jackson, and dealt in Manhattan real estate. As U.S. attorney for the southern district of New York, he was in the city when the Great Fire of 1835 hit, and he lit one of the fuses that blew up buildings to create a firebreak to help stop the blaze.

John Church He was an aide-de-camp to General William Henry Harrison in the War of 1812 and edited his father's writings.

William Stephen The son who looked the most like his father fought in the Black Hawk War and was a surveyor of public lands in Illinois before heading to California in the gold rush.

Eliza She married Sidney Holly; after his death, she lived with her mother and helped maintain her father's papers.

Philip "Little Phil" was an assistant U.S. attorney in New York and judge advocate of the U.S. Naval Retiring Board.

A 19TH-CENTURY ENGRAVING SHOWS THE MOMENT AT WHICH AARON BURR SHOT HAMILTON. ACCOUNTS DIFFER AS TO WHETHER HAMILTON EVEN TRIED TO FIRE HIS WEAPON BEFORE HE WAS SHOT.

honor. During the course of negotiations, each man insulted the other, making a duel unavoidable. On July 11, in Weehawken, New Jersey, the two men found themselves on a bluff with pistols drawn. Burr's shot pierced Hamilton's liver and lodged in his spine.

Hamilton knew he was done for. When Nathaniel Pendleton, his second, rushed to his side after the duel, Hamilton told him, "I am a dead man."

Perhaps with the tragedy of Philip's death in mind, Hamilton had taken pains to shield his family from the preparations for the duel. But there could be no avoiding the aftermath. Unaware that a duel had taken place, Eliza was blindsided by the news. She rushed to the house where her husband was staying and dissolved into tears at his bedside.

After Hamilton swore that he had never intended to do Burr harm in the duel, a priest agreed to give him Communion, and Hamilton said goodbye to his seven remaining children. He slipped away peacefully the next day.

For his part, Aaron Burr would never recover from the stain of the duel. Two shots were fired, but they occurred several seconds apart. A debate broke out, with Hamilton's allies insisting that Burr had shot first. Burr's supporters, on the other hand, were sure that Hamilton had fired first and Burr had responded. Although it remained unclear who shot first, it did not matter. Burr's political enemies were able to spin the duel as murder. In death, Hamilton had finally succeeded in ending Burr's political career.

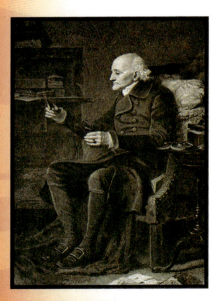

THOUGH BURR WAS NEVER TRIED ON MURDER CHARGES, THE DUEL CAST A PALL OVER THE REST OF HIS LIFE.

Eliza, who never remarried, found some comfort in a lock of hair clipped from her husband's head, and she wore around her neck a bag holding two papers: a sonnet Hamilton had written to woo her and a hymn he had left her on the morning of the duel. And as a new

A BUST OF HAMILTON SITS NEAR THE SPOT IN WEEHAWKEN, NEW JERSEY, WHERE HE WAS FATALLY WOUNDED.

generation of Americans came to regard the widow as a witness to history, she took pleasure in regaling them with fond memories of the man she called "my Hamilton."

The national outpouring of grief at Hamilton's death attests to his legacy. Although his vision of America's future was only one of many, its power—both to polarize and to energize—was undeniable, much like that of the man himself.

The Official Story

FOLLOWING THE DUEL, HAMILTON'S AND BURR'S SECONDS, NATHANIEL PENDLETON AND WILLIAM P. VAN NESS, WROTE AN OFFICIAL VERSION OF EVENTS. THE RECORD WAS PUBLISHED ON JULY 17, 1804, SIX DAYS AFTER THE DUEL.

Joint statement by William P. Van Ness and Nathaniel Pendleton on the duel between Alexander Hamilton and Aaron Burr

Col: Burr arrived first on the ground as had been previously agreed. When Genl Hamilton arrived the parties exchanged salutations and the Seconds proceeded to make their arrangments. They measured the distance, ten full paces, and cast lots for the choice of positions as also to determine by whom the word should be given, both of which fell to the Second of Genl Hamilton. They then proceeded to load the pistols in each others presence, after which the parties took their stations. The Gentleman who was to give the word, then explained to the parties the rules which were to govern them in firing which were as follows: The parties being placed at their stations The Second who gives the word shall ask them whether they are ready—being answered in the affirmative, he shall say "present" after which the parties shall present & fire when they please. If one fires before the other the opposite second shall say one two, three, fire, and he shall fire or loose his fire. And asked if they were prepared, being answered in the affirmative he gave the word present as had been agreed on, and both of the parties took aim, & fired in succession, the Intervening time is not expressed as the seconds do not precisely agree on that point. The pistols were discharged within a few seconds of each other and the fire of Col: Burr took effect; Genl Hamilton almost instantly fell. Col: Burr then advanced toward Genl H——n with a manner and gesture that appeared to Genl Hamilton's friend to be expressive of regret, but without Speaking turned about & withdrew. Being urged from the field by his friend as has been subsequently stated, with a view to prevent his being recognised by the Surgeon and Bargemen who were then approaching. No farther communications took place between the principals and the Barge that carried Col: Burr immediately returned to the City. We conceive it proper to add that the conduct of the parties in that interview was perfectly proper as suited the occasion.

106

ANOTHER 19TH-CENTURY ENGRAVING SHOWS HAMILTON FIRING CHIVALROUSLY INTO THE AIR AS BURR SHOOTS HIM.

THE FLINTLOCK PISTOLS BELONGING TO JOHN BARKER CHURCH SERVED NEITHER HIS BROTHER-IN-LAW NOR HIS NEPHEW WELL.

IN HIS OWN WORDS: ALEXANDER HAMILTON

A note on the speech bubbles in this book

Hamilton and his contemporaries really did say the things that appear in speech bubbles throughout this book, although the artwork does not necessarily depict the moment at which the statements were originally made.

Page 39

"Suspicion is the companion of mean souls, and the bane of all good society."

Thomas Paine wrote this in his pamphlet *Common Sense*, which caused a stir in the colonies when it was published in 1776. Paine criticized the British monarchy—saying that Britain had "groaned beneath" a large number of bad rulers—and went on to attack the idea of rule by monarchy altogether. He insisted that rule by Britain was inherently unfair for the colonies. In this quotation, Paine is defending the idea of religious tolerance. He goes on to say, "For myself, I fully and conscientiously believe, that it is the will of the

Almighty, that there should be a diversity of religious opinions among us: it affords a larger field for our Christian kindness."

Page 57
"Every post is honorable in which a man can serve his country."

George Washington wrote this in a letter to Colonel Benedict Arnold on September 14, 1775. The letter contained Washington's orders for Arnold to lead 1,200 men into Quebec, which had fallen under British control at the close of the French and Indian War. Washington gave Arnold detailed instructions on how to interact with the people of Quebec, as well as any other American forces he might encounter. He also dispensed advice for dealing with Arnold's own men, urging him to act to squelch the petty squabbling that often broke out among the officers about questions of rank, saying that all positions should be considered honorable when fighting in a just cause.

Five years later, Arnold, angry at being passed over for a promotion following his heroism at the Battle of Saratoga, would betray Washington by attempting to help the British capture the fort at West Point, New York.

Page 61
"The Nation which can prefer disgrace to danger is prepared for a Master and deserves one."

Alexander Hamilton wrote this in a letter that was published in the *Philadelphia Daily Advertiser* on February 21, 1797, entitled "The Warning No. III."

Following the French Revolution, the United States faced a dilemma. In 1778, France and the United States had signed a treaty of alliance, swearing to defend each other against aggression from Britain. When France declared war on Great Britain on January 31, 1793, Great Britain responded with a blockade of France. Many Americans believed that the U.S. should honor its earlier commitment to France. Many others, including Hamilton, did not. Hamilton argued that the original treaty of alliance had been signed with a monarch. Since that monarch had been dethroned in the French Revolution, the United States was no longer obligated to hold up its end of the alliance. Washington ultimately declared American neutrality in the conflict between France and Britain.

When the United States signed the Jay Treaty with Britain in 1795, France responded by pursuing and seizing American ships. Hamilton published a series of forceful letters, advocating that America defend its honor. In the third, he argued, "The honor of a nation is its life. Deliberately to abandon it is to commit an act of political suicide. There is treason in the sentiment avowed in the language of some, and betrayal by the conduct of others, that we ought to bear any thing from France rather than go to war with her. The Nation which can prefer disgrace to danger is prepared for a Master and deserves one."

Page 67

"No power on earth has a right to take our property from us without our consent."

John Jay wrote this in his "Address to the People of Britain," which was approved by the First Continental Congress on October 21, 1774. The address made an impassioned plea for the rights of the American colonies.

"Liberty may be endangered by the abuses of liberty, as well as by the abuses of power."

James Madison wrote this in one of his essays from *The Federalist*— no. 63. The essay is the second of a two-part defense of the Senate as it was established in the Constitution. In response to an imaginary heckler who might argue that the Senate could become a tyrannical body, he responded that for the Senate to run rampant it would have to not only become corrupt, but also manage to corrupt the House of Representatives and the state legislatures; and that abuses of liberty posed a greater threat to the United States than abuses of power.

Page 71

"Still I hope I shall always possess firmness and virtue enough to maintain . . . the character of an honest man."

George Washington wrote this to Alexander Hamilton on August 28, 1788. Washington was replying to a letter in which Hamilton had urged Washington to participate in the first presidential election. Washington would not express an interest in the presidency, insisting that he would prefer to live in retirement at Mount Vernon, saying, "it is my great and sole desire to live and die, in peace and retirement, on my own farm." Washington also wrote that he feared, if he became president, the world would accuse him of ambition and inconsistency. He defended his character, saying, "Still I hope I shall always possess firmness and virtue enough to maintain (what I consider the most enviable of all titles) the character of *an honest man.*"

Page 75

"A national debt if it is not excessive will be to us a national blessing."

Hamilton wrote this in a letter to Robert Morris on April 30, 1781. Morris had been nominated to the Continental Congress's department of finance. Hamilton responded to the news by sending Morris a letter of congratulations in which he included a lengthy discussion of banking and credit systems, made his case for a centralized national bank, and presented an outline for its structure.

Page 76

"The happiness of society is the end of government."

John Adams (who would later become the second president of the United States) wrote this in an essay entitled "Thoughts on Government" in April 1776. In response to a request from the North Carolina Provincial Congress, Adams gave his ideas about good government. He reflected on various ideas about the purpose of government, concluding that "Upon this point all speculative politicians will agree, that the happiness of society is the end of government, as all Divines and moral Philosophers will agree that the happiness of the individual is the end of man." The essay goes on to outline the need for checks and balances to prevent any one political body from becoming tyrannical.

"The whole art of government consists in the art of being honest."

Thomas Jefferson wrote this in July 1774 in an essay entitled "A Summary View of the Rights of British America."

Page 99

"The rule of my life is to make business a pleasure, and pleasure my business."

Aaron Burr, upholding his image as a scoundrel, wrote this in a letter to Louis André Pichon, a French diplomat. Pichon served as French ambassador to the United States during the Louisiana Purchase.

Page 103

"I am a dead man."

Hamilton reportedly knew that the wound he received would kill him. As his second, Nathaniel Pendleton, rushed to his side, Hamilton said, "I am a dead man." He was right, although he would not actually die until the following day.

Excerpts from the Writings of Alexander Hamilton

Alexander Hamilton was an almost obsessive writer. His work ranges from political tracts penned as a student at King's College to critical military letters delivered on behalf of General George Washington during his time as an aide-de-camp to notes sent to various associates that parsed local and national politics. And then, of course, there is the personal correspondence to family and friends. Taken together, the more than 6,000 letters and other writings available on the National Archives and Records Administration's Founders Online site (*founders.archives.gov*) chart not only his life but also the tumultuous birth of the United States, including Hamilton's many contributions to its form and direction. The documents touch on his troubled lineage, his search for love, and his frustrations with war. These excerpts, which are reprinted with Hamilton's abbreviations and misspellings intact, reveal a man of the Enlightenment whose thoughts transcended his time.

HAMILTON CHURNED OUT MANY OF HIS WRITINGS ON THIS LAP DESK.

Encouraging Washington to Run for President

November 18, 1788, to George Washington

Hamilton had previously urged his old commander to accept the presidency, suggesting in a letter in September 1788 that the "necessity of [Washington's] filling the station in question is so universal." His once and future boss was flattered by Hamilton's "frankness" and how he had "dealt thus freely and like a friend." In this letter of November 18, 1788, Hamilton continued to push, saying that "no other man can sufficiently unite the public opinion or can give the requisite weight to the office in the commencement of the Government." Further, Washington's refusal to accept "would have the worst effect imaginable." The rest is American history.

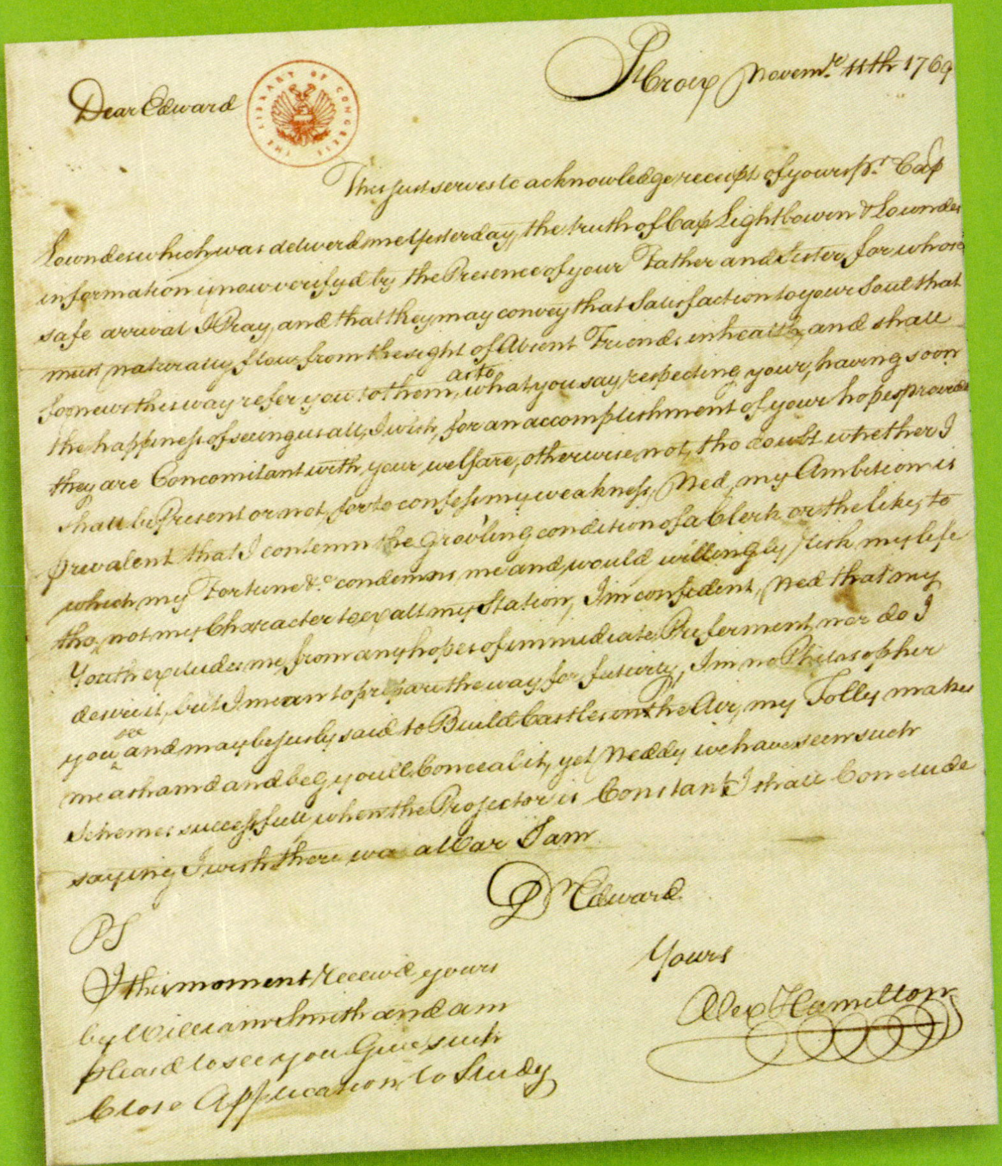

St Croix Novemr 11th 1769

Dear Edward

This just serves to acknowledge receipt of yours pr Cap Lowndes which was deliverd me Yesterday. The truth of Cap Lightbowen & Lowndes information is now verifyd by the Presence of your Father and Sister for whose safe arrival I Pray, and that they may convey that Satisfaction to your Soul that must naturally flow from the sight of Absent Friends in health, and shall for news this way refer you to them. As to what you say respecting your having soon the happiness of seeing us all, I wish, for an accomplishment of your hopes provided they are Concomitant with your welfare, otherwise not, tho doubt whether I shall be Present or not for to confess my weakness, Ned, my Ambition is prevalent that I contemn the grovling condition of a Clerk or the like, to which my Fortune &c. condemns me and would willingly risk my life tho' not my Character to exalt my Station. Im confident, Ned that my Youth excludes me from any hopes of immediate Preferment nor do I desire it, but I mean to prepare the way for futurity. Im no Philosopher you see and may be jusly said to Build Castles in the Air, my Folly makes me ashamd and beg youll Conceal it, yet Neddy we have seen such Schemes successfull when the Projector is Constant I shall Conclude saying I wish there was a War. I am

Dr Edward

Yours

Alex Hamilton

PS this moment receivd yours by William Smith and am pleasd to see you Give such Close Application to Study

A LETTER WRITTEN BY 12-YEAR-OLD HAMILTON IN 1769

On Recruiting Enslaved People for the Revolution

March 14, 1779, to John Jay

JOHN JAY

Hamilton had abhorred slavery since witnessing its brutality as a child in the Caribbean. Four years into the American Revolution, he suggested to Jay, president of the Continental Congress, that enslaved people be allowed to enlist in the fight against the British. And he recommended they be granted their freedom in return for their service.

I mention this, because I frequently hear it objected to the scheme of embodying negroes that they are too stupid to make soldiers. This is so far from appearing to me a valid objection that I think their want of cultivation (for their natural faculties are probably as good as ours) joined to that habit of subordination which they acquire from a life of servitude, will make them sooner became soldiers than our White inhabitants. Let officers be men of sense and sentiment, and the nearer the soldiers approach to machines perhaps the better.

I foresee that this project will have to combat much opposition from prejudice and self-interest. The contempt we have been taught to entertain for the blacks, makes us fancy many things that are founded neither in reason nor experience; and an unwillingness to part with property of so valuable a kind will furnish a thousand arguments to show the impracticability or pernicious tendency of a scheme which requires such a sacrifice. . . . An essential part of the plan is to give them their freedom with their muskets. This will secure their fidelity, animate their courage, and I believe will have a good influence upon those who remain, by opening a door to their emancipation.

On the Search for a Wife

April 1779 to John Laurens

JOHN LAURENS

Laurens, who joined General Washington's staff in 1777, eventually became Hamilton's closest friend. In the spring of 1779, he was headed to South Carolina, and the 24-year-old Hamilton asked that Laurens find him a mate while he was there. His wish list of required attributes was impressively long.

And Now my Dear as we are upon the subject of wife, I empower and command you to get me one in Carolina. . . . She must be young, handsome (I lay most stress upon a good shape) sensible (a little learning will do), well bred (but she must have an aversion to the word ton) chaste and tender (I am an enthusiast in my notions of fidelity and fondness) of some good nature, a great deal of generosity (she must neither love money nor scolding, for I dislike equally a termagent and an œconomist). In politics, I am indifferent what side she may be of; I think I have arguments that will easily convert her to mine. As to religion a moderate stock will satisfy me. She must believe in god and hate a saint. But as to fortune, the larger stock of that the better. . . .

If you should not readily meet with a lady that you think answers my description you can only advertise in the public papers. . . . To excite their emulation, it will be necessary for you to give an account of the lover—his size, make, quality of mind and body, achievements, expectations, fortune, &c. In drawing my picture, you will no doubt be civil to your friend; mind you do justice to the length of my nose.

On the Misery of War

September 12, 1780, to John Laurens

By the late summer of 1780, the Continental Army had been fighting the British for five long years. Hamilton, clearly worn down by the rigors of the campaign, needed to vent to someone about the unending struggle and its unyielding hardships.

You can hardly conceive in how dreadful a situation we are. The army, in the course of the present month, has received only four or five days rations of meal, and we really know not of any adequate relief in future. This distress at such a stage of the campaign sours the soldiery. 'Tis in vain you make apologies to them. The officers are out of humour, and the worst of evils seems to be coming upon us—a loss of our virtue. . . . The truth is I am an unlucky honest man, that speak my sentiments to all and with emphasis. I say this to you because you know it and will not charge me with vanity. I hate Congress—I hate the army—I hate the world—I hate myself. The whole is a mass of fools and knaves.

On the Ratification Debate

October 11, 1787, to George Washington

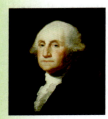

GEORGE WASHINGTON

Once the delegates in Philadelphia had created the new Constitution, it had to be ratified by the states. Hamilton took the opportunity to inform his former commander about what he expected to be an arduous process—and sent a copy of a piece he had written attacking the anti-Federalist New York Governor George Clinton.

The New Constitution is as popular in this City as it is possible for any thing to be—and the prospect thus far is favourable to it throughout the state. But there is no saying what turn things may take when the full flood of official influence is let loose against it. This is to be expected, for, though the Governor has not publicly declared himself, his particular connections and confidential friends are loud against it.

On His Distrust of Aaron Burr

September 21, 1792, to an unknown recipient

AARON BURR

In 1789, Hamilton's father-in-law, General Philip Schuyler, became one of New York's first two senators. When Schuyler, a Federalist, ran for re-election, anti-Federalist opponents nominated Burr to replace him. When Burr's campaign succeeded, it made a lifelong enemy of Hamilton. Here, he makes his feelings toward Burr abundantly clear.

I fear the other Gentleman [Burr] is unprincipled both as a public and private man. When the constitution was in deliberation, his conduct was equivocal; but its enemies, who I believe best understood him considered him as with them. In fact, I take it, he is for or against nothing, but as it suits his interest or ambition. He is determined, as I conceive, to make his way to be the head of the popular party and to climb per fas et nefas to the highest honors of the state; and as much higher as circumstances may permit. Embarrassed, as I understand, in his circumstances, with an extravagant family—bold enterprising and intriguing, I am mistaken, if it be not his object to play the game of confusion, and I feel it a religious duty to oppose his career.

On the Affair

July 1797 in a pamphlet

In *Observations on Certain Documents Contained in No. V & VI of "The History of the United States for the Year 1796," In Which the Charge of Speculation Against Alexander Hamilton, Late Secretary of the Treasury, is Fully Refuted. Written by Himself,* Hamilton sought to get ahead of the damage brought on by revelations of his affair with Maria Reynolds. By responding so forthrightly to accusations not only about the relationship but also of financial wrongdoing, he hoped to show he had nothing to hide. An implication that Maria and her husband had planned the entanglement as a blackmail ploy from the beginning couldn't have hurt.

The charge against me is a connection with one James Reynolds for purposes of improper pecuniary speculation. My real crime is an amorous connection with his wife, for a considerable time with his privity and connivance, if not originally brought on by a combination between the husband and wife with the design to extort money from me.

This confession is not made without a blush. I cannot be the apologist of any vice because the ardour of passion may have made it mine. I can never cease to condemn myself for the pang, which it may inflict in a bosom eminently intitled to all my gratitude, fidelity and love. But that bosom will approve, that even at so great an expence, I should effectually wipe away a more serious stain from a name, which it cherishes with no less elevation than tenderness. The public too will I trust excuse the confession. The necessity of it to my defence against a more heinous charge could alone have extorted from me so painful an indecorum.

On His Past

August 26, 1800, to William Jackson

WILLIAM JACKSON

Hamilton and Jackson were old friends, having worked together on Washington's staff during the war. Jackson and John Laurens went to Paris in 1781 to see about getting a loan and supplies from France, and Jackson served as secretary of the Constitutional Convention. He and Hamilton were so close that Hamilton entrusted Jackson with information about his affair with Maria Reynolds, and here with "the real history" of his ancestry and birth. It was a topic that clearly still pained him as an adult.

Never was there a more ungenerous persecution of any man than of myself.—Not only the worst constructions are put upon my conduct as a public man but it seems my birth is the subject of the most humiliating criticism. . . .

I think it proper to confide to your bosom the real history of it, that among my friends you may if you please wipe off some part of the stain which is so industriously impressed. . . .

My Grandfather by the mothers side of the name of Faucette was a French Huguenot who emigrated to the West Indies in consequence of the revocation of the Edict of Nantz and settled in the Island of Nevis and there acquired a pretty fortune. I have been assured by persons who knew him that he was a man of letters and much of a gentleman. He practiced a[s] a Physician, whether that was his original profession, or one assumed for livelihood after his emigration is not to me ascertained.

My father now dead was certainly of a respectable Scotch Fami[ly.] His father was, and the son of his Eldest brother now is Laird of Grang[e.] His mother was the sister of an ancient Baronet Sir Robert Pollock.

. . . For some time he was supported by his friends in Scotland, and for several years before his death by me. It was his fault to have had too much pride and two large a portion of indolence—but his character was otherwise without reproach and his manners those of a Gentleman.

On His Son's Death

February 29, 1802, to Gouverneur Morris

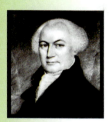

GOUVERNEUR MORRIS

In 1801, George Eacker gave a speech against Hamilton, and Hamilton's eldest son, Philip, and a friend, Richard Price, taunted the lawyer about it. Eacker branded the men "a set of rascals," and two duels were set. On November 22, Price and Eacker faced off in Paulus Hook, New Jersey. Neither was hit. The next day, it was Hamilton's turn. This time, Eacker's bullet struck its target, above the hip. The 19-year-old died the following day. The passing of his son devastated Hamilton and the family. Months later, Morris, at the time serving in the U.S. Senate, received word of his friend's profoundly unsettled state.

Mine is an odd destiny. Perhaps no man in the UStates has sacrificed or done more for the present Constitution than myself—and contrary to all my anticipations of its fate, as you know from the very begginning I am still labouring to prop the frail and worthless fabric. Yet I have the murmurs of its friends no less than the curses of its foes for my rewards. What can I do better than withdraw from the Scene? Every day proves to me more and more that this American world was not made for me.

On His Own Death

July 4, 1804, to Elizabeth Hamilton

ELIZABETH HAMILTON

Both Hamilton and Burr kept their upcoming duel a secret from their families. Still, each man prepared letters in case he was killed. Burr wrote to his beloved daughter Theodosia Burr Alston: "I am indebted to you, my dearest Theodosia, for a very great portion of the happiness which I have enjoyed in this life. You have completely satisfied all that my heart and affections had hoped or even wished. . . . Adieu. Adieu." Hamilton penned a similar farewell to his wife. He died the following week.

This letter, my very dear Eliza, will not be delivered to you, unless I shall first have terminated my earthly career; to begin, as I humbly hope from redeeming grace and divine mercy, a happy immortality.

If it had been possible for me to have avoided the interview, my love for you and my precious children would have been alone a decisive motive. But it was not possible, without sacrifices which would have rendered me unworthy of your esteem. I need not tell you of the pangs I feel, from the idea of quitting you and exposing you to the anguish which I know you would feel. Nor could I dwell on the topic lest it should unman me.

The consolations of Religion, my beloved, can alone support you; and these you have a right to enjoy. Fly to the bosom of your God and be comforted. With my last idea; I shall cherish the sweet hope of meeting you in a better world.

Adieu best of wives and best of Women. Embrace all my darling Children for me.

Alexander Hamilton

The Life and Times of Alexander Hamilton

1755

JANUARY 11—ALEXANDER HAMILTON WAS BORN.

1765

JULY—THE SONS OF LIBERTY, A COVERT GROUP OF COLONISTS LED BY SAMUEL ADAMS, FORMED IN OPPOSITION TO THE STAMP ACT.

1764

SEPTEMBER 1—THE CURRENCY ACT, WHICH PROHIBITED COLONIES FROM ISSUING THEIR OWN PAPER MONEY, WAS PASSED BY THE BRITISH PARLIAMENT.

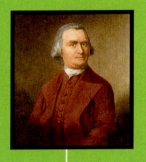

| 1755 | 1755 | 1764 | 1765 | 1765 | 1768 |

1768

FEBRUARY 19—RACHEL FAUCETTE LAVIEN DIED.

1755

FEBRUARY—GEORGE WASHINGTON JOINED A COLUMN OF 2,100 MEN WHO MARCHED INTO THE OHIO TERRITORY IN A BID AGAINST THE FRENCH. TAKING OVER AFTER HIS GENERAL WAS KILLED, WASHINGTON IMPOSED ORDER AND LED 977 SURVIVORS TO SAFETY.

1765

MARCH—PARLIAMENT PASSED THE STAMP ACT AND THE QUARTERING ACT.

1772

OCTOBER 3—
THE ROYAL
DANISH AMERICAN
GAZETTE RAN
HAMILTON'S
"HURRICANE
LETTER."
IMPRESSED
LOCAL
DIGNITARIES
UNDERWROTE
THE TEEN'S
IMMIGRATION
TO AMERICA TO
FURTHER HIS
EDUCATION.

1773

DECEMBER 16—BOSTON TEA PARTY.

1774

SEPTEMBER 5—THE
FIRST CONTINENTAL
CONGRESS CONVENED
IN PHILADELPHIA.

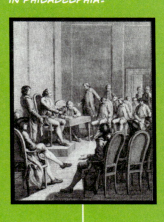

1772   1773   1773   1773   1774   1775 >

1773

MAY 10—PARLIAMENT'S
TEA ACT LOWERED
THE PRICE OF TEA IN
THE COLONIES BUT
CONFIRMED THEIR LACK
OF REPRESENTATION.

1773

SUMMER—
HAMILTON MOVED
IN WITH WILLIAM
LIVINGSTON'S FAMILY
IN ELIZABETHTOWN,
NEW JERSEY. A FEW
MONTHS LATER, HE
ENROLLED AT KING'S
COLLEGE.

1775

APRIL 18—PAUL REVERE'S RIDE.

1775

JUNE 19—GEORGE WASHINGTON BECAME COMMANDER IN CHIEF OF THE CONTINENTAL ARMY.

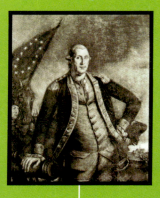

1776

MARCH 14—HAMILTON ENLISTED AND RECEIVED A COMMISSION: ARTILLERY COMPANY CAPTAIN.

1780

DECEMBER 14—HAMILTON MARRIED ELIZABETH SCHUYLER.

1775 **1775** **1776** **1776** **1777** **1780**

1775

APRIL 19—THE REVOLUTIONARY WAR BEGAN WITH CLASHES IN THE MASSACHUSETTS COLONY TOWNS OF LEXINGTON AND CONCORD.

1776

JULY 4—THE DECLARATION OF INDEPENDENCE WAS SIGNED.

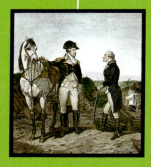

1777

MARCH 1—HAMILTON JOINED WASHINGTON AS AN AIDE-DE-CAMP WITH THE RANK OF LIEUTENANT COLONEL.

1781

FEBRUARY—HAMILTON RESIGNED HIS POSITION WITH WASHINGTON.

1781

MAY 17—AFTER BEING NAMED THE U.S. SUPERINTENDENT OF FINANCE, ROBERT MORRIS SUBMITTED A PLAN FOR A NATIONAL BANK OF NORTH AMERICA.

1781

OCTOBER 19—HAMILTON LED HIS MEN IN A CHARGE TO SEIZE A STRATEGIC REDOUBT DURING THE BATTLE OF YORKTOWN.

1781   **1781**   **1781**   **1781**   **1781**   **1782 >**

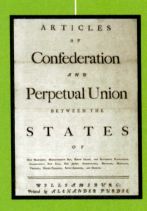

1782

JULY—HAMILTON WAS ADMITTED TO THE NEW YORK STATE BAR.

1781

MARCH 1—THE ARTICLES OF CONFEDERATION WENT INTO EFFECT.

1781

JULY—WASHINGTON AWARDED HAMILTON COMMAND OF A LIGHT-INFANTRY BATTALION IN THE MARQUIS DE LAFAYETTE'S CORPS.

1783
SEPTEMBER 3—THE TREATY OF PARIS WAS SIGNED, OFFICIALLY ENDING THE REVOLUTIONARY WAR.

1786
SEPTEMBER—AT A REGIONAL MEETING IN ANNAPOLIS, MARYLAND, HAMILTON PROPOSED A FEDERAL CONVENTION TO REVISE THE ARTICLES OF CONFEDERATION.

1782 **1783** **1786** **1787** **1788**

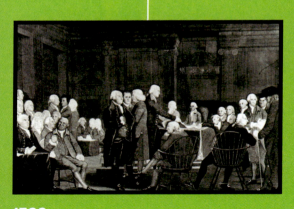

1787
SEPTEMBER 17— THE U.S. CONSTITUTION WAS SIGNED.

1782
OCTOBER 25—HAMILTON WAS NAMED A NEW YORK DELEGATE TO THE CONTINENTAL CONGRESS.

1788
THE FEDERALIST ESSAYS ARE PUBLISHED IN TWO BOUND EDITIONS.

1789
APRIL 30—WASHINGTON TOOK THE OATH OF OFFICE AS THE NATION'S FIRST PRESIDENT.

1791
DECEMBER 5—HAMILTON SUBMITTED HIS "REPORT ON MANUFACTURES."

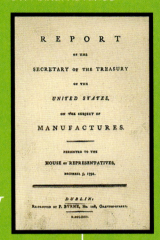

1790
DECEMBER 14—HAMILTON PRESENTED THE SECOND "REPORT ON THE PUBLIC CREDIT," IN WHICH HE URGED THE CREATION OF A BANK OF THE UNITED STATES.

1789   1789   1790   1790   1791   1791 >

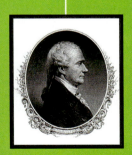

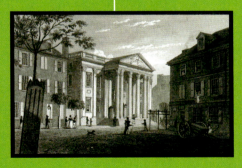

1789
SEPTEMBER 11—HAMILTON WAS APPOINTED THE FIRST U.S. SECRETARY OF THE TREASURY.

1790
JANUARY 14—IN THE FIRST OF TWO "REPORTS ON THE PUBLIC CREDIT," HAMILTON PROPOSED THAT THE FEDERAL GOVERNMENT FUND THE NATIONAL DEBT.

1791
FEBRUARY 25—WASHINGTON APPROVED HAMILTON'S NATIONAL BANK PLAN.

1800

IN RESPONSE TO AN INSULT, HAMILTON PUBLISHED A 54-PAGE PAMPHLET ATTACKING PRESIDENT JOHN ADAMS.

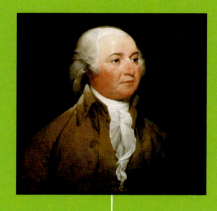

1795

JANUARY 31— HAMILTON RESIGNED AS TREASURY SECRETARY.

1800

JUNE 15— HAMILTON RESIGNED AS INSPECTOR GENERAL.

1795 **1797** **1798** **1800** **1800** **1801**

1798

WASHINGTON APPOINTED HAMILTON AS THE COUNTRY'S INSPECTOR GENERAL, SECOND-IN-COMMAND OF THE U.S. ARMY.

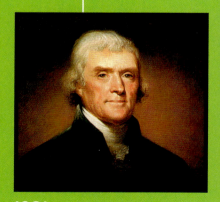

1797

SUMMER—HAMILTON RELEASED A 95-PAGE TELL-ALL PAMPHLET TO GET AHEAD OF WHAT BECAME AMERICA'S FIRST SEX SCANDAL.

1801

FEBRUARY 11—PRESIDENTIAL CANDIDATES THOMAS JEFFERSON AND AARON BURR DEADLOCKED IN THE ELECTORAL COLLEGE.

1801

NOVEMBER 16—THE NEW-YORK EVENING POST, WHICH HAMILTON HELPED FOUND, PUBLISHED ITS FIRST EDITION.

1802

SUMMER—CONSTRUCTION WAS COMPLETED ON HAMILTON'S DREAM HOUSE, THE GRANGE, IN MANHATTAN.

1804

JULY 11—HAMILTON AND BURR DUELED.

| 1801 | 1801 | 1802 | 1803 | 1804 | 1804 |

1801

NOVEMBER 22—PHILIP, HAMILTON'S ELDEST SON, WAS MORTALLY WOUNDED WHILE DEFENDING HIS FATHER'S HONOR IN A DUEL WITH GEORGE EACKER.

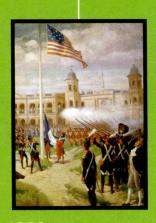

1803

APRIL 30—THE LOUISIANA PURCHASE TREATY WAS SIGNED.

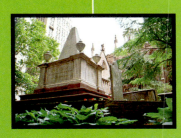

1804

JULY 12—HAMILTON DIED.

INDEX

Page numbers in **bold** refer to illustrations.

ACKNOWLEDGMENTS

The text in this book was adapted from content originally published in *Alexander Hamilton: A Founding Father's Visionary Genius and His Tragic Fate*, New York: Time Inc. Books, 2015; and includes work by Sarah Begley, Joanne B. Freeman, Daniel S. Levy, Christopher Matthews, Courtney Mifsud, Lily Rothman, and Ellen Trumposky.

PICTURE CREDITS

Cover: Tim O'Brien

Pages 1: National Numismatic Collection/Smithsonian Institution; **3:** National Numismatic Collection/Smithsonian Institution; **4:** NMUIM/Alamy; **6:** Tim O'Brien; **7:** Universal History Archive/UIG/Getty Images; **8:** (top) The Granger Collection, (bottom) Stuart Forster/REX/Shutterstock; **9:** New York Historical Society; **10:** Tim O'Brien; **11:** George H. H. Huey/Alamy; **12:** French School/Getty Images; **13:** Archive Farms/Getty Images; **15:** Don Hebert/Stockbyte/Getty Images; **16–17:** Getty Images; **20:** The Granger Collection; **22:** (top) Duncan1890/Getty Images; (bottom) New York Historical Society/Getty Images; **24:** Library of Congress; **25:** Robert J. Hill/Getty Images; **26:** Library of Congress (2); **27:** (top) Wikipedia, (bottom) DeAgostini/Getty Images; **28:** Tim O'Brien; **29:** North Wind Picture Archives/Alamy; **30:** (left) Fine Art Images/Heritage Images/Getty Images, (center left, right) DeAgostini/Getty Images, (center right) Fine Art Images/Heritage Images/Getty Images; **31:** New York Historical Society/Getty Images; **32:** GraphicaArtis/Getty Images; **33:** Chronicle/Alamy; **34–35:** 3LH/SuperStock; **37:** Bettmann/Getty Images; **38:** Library and Archives Canada; **39:** (top) National Gallery of Art, (bottom) Library of Congress; **41:** National Archives; **42, 43:** Joan Marcus (3); **44:** Tim O'Brien; **45, 47:** North Wind Picture Archives/Alamy; **49:** Clarence Holmes/Alamy; **50:** Time Life Pictures/Mansell/The LIFE Picture Collection/Getty Images; **51:** The Granger Collection; **55:** Corbis/Getty Images; **56–57:** Architect of the Capitol; **58:** (top) The Granger Collection, (bottom) Bettmann/Getty Images; **59:** (top) Library of Congress, (middle) Beinecke Rare Book and Manuscript Library/Yale University, (bottom) The Granger Collection; **60:** Tim O'Brien; **61:** Universal History Archive/UIG/Getty Images; **63:** Stock Montage/Getty Images; **65:** The Granger Collection (2); **66:** MPI/Getty Images; **67:** (left) DeAgostini/Getty Images, (right) GraphicaArtis/Getty Images; **68:** National Archives; **70:** Mount Vernon Ladies' Association; **71:** Stock Montage/Getty Images; **72:** (top) Library of Congress, (bottom) The Granger Collection; **73:** (top) Wikipedia, (bottom) Getty Images; **74:** Tim O'Brien; **75:** Ian Dagnall/Alamy; **76:** (left) Hi-Story/Alamy, (right) Bettmann/Getty Images; **80:** Corbis/Getty Images; **81:** National Numismatic Collection/Smithsonian Institution; **83:** Library of Congress; **85:** Universal History Archive/Getty Images; **86–87:** Ron Rovtar/Alamy; **88:** (top 4) National Numismatic Collection/Smithsonian Institution; (bottom) Nick Fielding/Alamy; **89:** (Earhart) The Seattle Times/JR Partners/Getty Images; (Parks) Don Cravens/The LIFE Images Collection/Getty Images; (Roosevelt) Stock Montage/Getty Images; (Tubman) Ann Ronan/Print Collector/Getty Images; **90:** Tim O'Brien; **91:** Lee Snider/Corbis/Getty Images; **94:** Stefano Giovannini ; **95:** Library of Congress; **96:** (top) Harry Warnecke/New York Daily News Archive/Getty Images, (bottom) Andrew Henderson/The New York Times/Redux; **97:** (top) Stefano Giovannini, (bottom) Joshua Bright/The New York Times/Redux; **98:** Tim O'Brien; **99:** The Granger Collection; **103:** North Wind Picture Archives/Alamy; **104:** Chronicle/Alamy; **105:** Dennis K. Johnson/Lonely Planet Images/ Getty Images; **106:** Getty Images; **107:** (top) Library of Congress, (bottom) The Granger Collection; **115:** Stefano Giovannini; **116:** Library of Congress; **117:** Kean Collection/Getty Images; **118:** Smith Collection/Gado/Getty Images; **120:** Photo12/UIG/Getty Images; **121:** Hulton Archive/Getty Images; **122:** Beinecke Rare Book and Manuscript Library/Yale University; **123:** Kean Collection/Getty Images; **125:** Corbis/Getty Images; **126:** The Granger Collection; **127:** Smith Collection/Gado/Getty Images.

Timeline: (1755 Hamilton birthplace) Tony Roberts/Getty Images, (1755 George Washington) PhotoQuest/Getty Images, (1765 stamp) New York Historical Society/Getty Images, (1765 Sons of Liberty)/ Stock Montage/Getty Images, (1773 Tea Act) Hulton Archive/Getty Images, (1773 King's College) North Wind Picture Archives/Alamy, (1773 Boston Tea Party) GraphicaArtis/Getty Images, (1774) MPI/Getty Images, (1775 Paul Revere) Ed Vebell/Getty Images, (1775 Minutemen) Hulton Archive/Getty Images, (1775 Washington) Universal History Archive/UIG/Getty Images, (1776 Hamilton) North Wind Picture Archives/Alamy, (1776 Declaration) National Archives, (1777) North Wind Picture Archives/Alamy, (1780) Kean Collection/Getty Images; (1781 Articles of Confederation) Library of Congress, (1781 Robert Morris) Stock Montage/Getty Images, (1781 Marquis de Lafayette) Imagno/Getty Images, (1781 Battle of Yorktown) Ann Ronan Pictures/Print Collector/Getty Images, (1782) Hulton Archive/Getty Images, (1783) Corbis/Getty Images, (1786) MPI/Getty Images, (1787) National Archives, (1788) Library of Congress, (1789 Washington) Photo12/UIG/Getty Images, (1789 Hamilton) The Bureau of Engraving and Printing/U.S. Government, (1790) Library of Congress, (1791 bank) Kean Collection/Getty Images, (1791 Observations pamphlet) Beinecke Rare Book and Manuscript Library/Yale University, (1791 report) The Granger Collection, (1800) GraphicaArtis/Getty Images, (1801 Jefferson) GraphicaArtis/Getty Images, (1801 Philip Hamilton) The Granger Collection, (1802) Library of Congress, (1803) Wikimedia, (1804 duel) Universal History Archive/UIG/Getty Images, (1804 Hamilton tomb) Patti McConville/Alamy.